To Bill , + Sharon
in love

[signature]

PENTECOST REKINDLED

R. Glenn Brown

Port Hole Publications
Florence, Oregon

ISBN-13: 978-0-9892608-5-5
ISBN-10: 0-9892608-5-2
Copyright 2014 by Glenn Brown
Bible quotations taken from the New International Version
Cover Design by Ruth Kirkpatrick
All Rights Reserved
Published by Port Hole Publications
179 Laurel St. – Suite D
Florence, Oregon 97439
Website: portholepublications.com

DEDICATION

This book is lovingly dedicated to the multitudes of sincere Christians who hunger for more of the presence and power of the Holy Spirit but are fearful of becoming part of something extra-biblical and divisive.

May this book encourage you in your search for the genuine and true.

CONTENTS

PREFACE

This book continues a theological dialogue that I publicly entered when I wrote and published my first book *PENTECOST REVISITED*. I continue to confront the division within the body of Christ between traditional Pentecostalism and the broader Evangelical community. I particularly focus upon the distinctive doctrine of the Assemblies of God, the church in which I was reared and in which I served for fifty-two years as an ordained pastor, Navy chaplain and missionary. As a consequence of publishing *PENTECOST REVISITED,* I resigned from my denomination in 2010 and am now associated with *CHAPLAINCY FULL GOSPEL CHURCHES* in Dallas, Texas.

I have deep affection for the church I served for over half a century. There are friendships formed over the years in this fellowship that cannot be broken by doctrinal disputes. The centrality of our common faith in Jesus Christ has never been in dispute. What is in dispute is the hardened Pentecostal tradition that there is no valid Spirit baptism unless initially evidenced by speaking in tongues. I believe I demonstrate conclusively from Scripture that this is erroneous teaching and has created needless division and sometimes personal havoc.

But I go beyond that and point out the positive reasons why speaking in tongues accompanied the outpouring of the Spirit at Pentecost. Those positive reasons apply to speaking in tongues today but they are totally ignored by traditional Pentecostals and traditional Evangelicals alike. When they are recognized and applied they can become a powerful unifying force within a fractured church. These biblical purposes I see more clearly now than I did when I wrote *PENTECOST REVISITED.* I am eager to share them with you in *PENTECOST REKINDLED.*

Millions of sincere Christians have been reluctant to seek the fullness of the Holy Spirit because of the unscriptural teaching that links Spirit baptism with speaking in tongues. These earnest believers have enough biblical insight and maturity to know this teaching is without foundation in scripture. But beware! Reject false teaching concerning the purpose of tongues but don't toss away the baptism in the Holy Spirit.

Because the Holy Spirit is called the neglected member of the Trinity, let me inject a brief explanation about Spirit baptism. The baptism in the Holy Spirit is distinct from regeneration. In regeneration the Holy Spirit is the active divine Agent who baptizes (immerses) believers into the body of Christ (I Corinthians 12:13). In Spirit baptism Jesus Christ is the divine Agent who baptizes (immerses) believers into the Holy Spirit, just as John and Jesus predicted (Luke 3:16; Acts 1:5). The purpose of this baptism is to provide spiritual power to fulfill your part of the mission that will advance the kingdom of God on earth. Since Jesus is the sovereign Baptizer it seems unduly arrogant to attempt to tell him how he must do his work.

The teaching that every valid Spirit baptism must be evidenced by speaking in tongues is the hallmark of American Pentecostals. It was Dr. Allan Anderson, a personal friend and Professor of Global Pentecostal Studies at University of Birmingham (UK), who made me aware that, world-wide, multitudes of Pentecostals and/or Charismatics do not insist on tongues as required evidence of valid Spirit baptism. In much of the world, the term *Pentecostal/Charismatic* is seen as "referring to those movements with an emphasis on the experience of the power of the Holy Spirit with accompanying manifestations of the imminent presence of God." (Allan Anderson) My heart and mind concurs with this conclusion. *PENTECOST REKINDLED* leads in that direction and helps us arrive there, united in Jesus Christ.

For the multitude of Christians who have never spoken in tongues but have a passionate hunger for God's powerful presence, let me say unequivocally and categorically: "You can be baptized in the Holy Spirit without tongues."

Speaking in tongues is one of the spiritual gifts which the Holy Spirit may or may not impart to you. But it is not a sign that you have been baptized in the Spirit or filled with the Spirit, although it may accompany this experience. (The first time one is filled with the Holy Spirit is often referred to as the time when the individual is "baptized in the Spirit".) "Baptized" and "filled" are used interchangeably in the New Testament. (Compare Acts 1:5 with Acts 2:4 ; 4:31.)

Without this empowering experience the church is impotent.

But don't seek an experience. Seek God and let Him determine the way He manifests His empowering presence. He will tailor your experience to your unique personality and potential. Trust Him.

R. Glenn Brown
Sequim, WA

CHAPTER 1

THE JOURNEY BEGINS

On April 23, 2008, at the annual Council of the Northern California/Nevada District of the Assemblies of God, I was recognized for a half century of ordained ministry with my church and awarded the fifty-year lapel pin. The last 38 years had been in fellowship with that great district. I respected its outstanding leadership over all the years I had been affiliated. I loved my association there as a Navy chaplain, pastor and missionary. I treasure ties of friendship that will endure into eternity.

Two years later I submitted a letter of resignation from the Assemblies of God to my respected District Superintendent, Jim Braddy. Over the years, as a result of extensive study of Scripture, I had become convinced that my church erred in its insistence that every valid Spirit baptism must be evidenced by speaking in tongues.

Speaking in tongues was not the issue. I knew Scripture clearly taught this was one of the gifts of the Spirit that had been dramatically displayed at Pentecost. The issue was the erroneous purpose that we Pentecostals had assigned to tongues that conflicted with Scripture. I discovered that the Bible displays a unique purpose for tongues meant to motivate evangelism and promote unity. It took me years to make this discovery. My spiritual pilgrimage is described in the pages that follow. Whatever your religious persuasion, I believe you will find this journey one which will challenge you to seek for truth earnestly and fearlessly.

I was reared in a Pentecostal preacher's home, the oldest of eleven children. Before I was born, my parents had been traveling evangelists taking the exciting message of the Pentecostal renewal to Kansas, Oklahoma and Arkansas. They and another young couple traveled in twin, custom-made motor homes with the sign "JESUS SAVES" boldly emblazoned across the front of the body above the windshield. They didn't call such vehicles "motor homes" eighty-five years ago. They were known as "truck houses" and most were built on a Model T Ford truck chassis.

Sometime before my birth my parents parked the truck house

and rented a small ranch in northwestern Kansas. My dad had grown up on a wheat farm and cattle ranch. I was born January 7, 1928, in Norton County near the southern Nebraska border. The doctor had to fight his way through a snowstorm to reach the house and assist my mother in the birth of her firstborn.

My life started in western Kansas, but a combination of horrific dust storms, plagues of grasshoppers and jackrabbits, and a deepening economic depression influenced my parents to migrate to North Carolina. All these factors influenced their move, but what really motivated them to action was the conviction that God had called them to respond to an invitation to establish a new Pentecostal church near Reidsville, North Carolina.

In July 1935, my parents loaded my two-year-old brother, Johnny, and me into the Model T motor home and embarked on a cross-country adventure. It was great fun for a seven-year-old boy! Sometimes, on long or steep uphill inclines, the engine would grind to a halt. Mama would say, "Glenny, grab a chock and help me block the wheels." Then Mama and I would put chocks behind the back wheels. Daddy would rev up the engine, let out the clutch and we would surge forward. This would be repeated until we conquered the incline.

We arrived in North Carolina and, after two years of hard work and perseverance by my parents, a congregation was established and a church erected near Reidsville. The first of my six sisters was born there. In 1937 we moved again and daddy began a series of pastorates in established Pentecostal churches. The first was in Mt. Hope, West Virginia (1937-39), where my brother Charles was born. We then moved to Williamstown, West Virginia (1939-41), where another sister was born. And then we moved to Cedar Bluff, Virginia (1942-44), where two more sisters were born.

While I was growing up, dad pastored each church for a relatively short time of two or three years. Why did we move so often? I am not sure but my guess is that he was hoping to find a larger church that could more adequately support our growing family. Dad resigned from the Cedar Bluff church in November, 1944, and engaged in evangelism for a year before securing a pastorate in Morganton, North Carolina, where he stayed for the next eleven years. During this time two more sisters and our youngest brother, Philip, were born.

When the family moved to Morganton I stayed in my high school and graduated with my class. Although I loved my parents dearly and cared deeply about my younger siblings, I was eager to break free of parental restrictions.

The churches as a whole in our area of the South, Pentecostal churches in particular, were steeped in legalistic morality. My dad didn't want me to be involved in competitive sports because they were "worldly" but, with mama's gentle urging, he reluctantly permitted me to play football and basketball. I was the star basketball player for the high school in my senior year but Dad never attended any of our games. This stifling, stringent, strict expression of Christianity never appealed to me. I had hoped to make a career in athletics as a coach. How could I be a Christian and a coach if participating in competitive sports disqualified me? I decided this kind of faith was not for me.

I must say in defense of my preacher dad, he outgrew this legalistic straight jacket. Years later he and Johnny and I enjoyed playing golf together. He became a fierce competitor in the family game of Rook in which "sanctified" numbered cards were substituted for standard playing cards. My fun-loving mother and a houseful of active youngsters helped liberate him! But his freedom came after I had left the family circle, although I enjoyed the results of it for many years.

YOU'RE IN THE ARMY NOW

I wanted very much to attend college but lacked money. I ended up spending the summer after graduation from high school harvesting wheat in Kansas and Colorado on my uncles' farms. Upon returning to my parents' home in North Carolina, I announced that I wanted to enlist in the Army Air Corps. This would make me eligible for the GI Bill which would be my scholarship to college.

Despite the protestations of my parents, on October 4, 1946, I reported to the Army recruiter in Morganton, North Carolina, and declared my intention to enlist in the U.S. Army Air Corps. Four days later I was sworn in at Fort Bragg, North Carolina. Within two weeks I was undergoing basic training near San Antonio, Texas.

After basic I was assigned to Randolph Field, also near San Antonio. Not long after arriving, I was selected to attend Photography School at Lowry Field near Denver, Colorado. After completing photo school I returned to Randolph Field and was assigned to the Army Air Corp Film Strip Preparation Center. It was a great job for a teenager. One of the best things about it was that my work schedule permitted me to enroll in night classes at Trinity University. Uncle Sam paid for the tuition and books. I had to pay bus fare from the base to the university campus, but even a Corporal could afford that.

A SEASON FOR QUESTIONING

My evenings at Trinity University helped speed a spiritual crisis in my life. Three years had passed since I had declared my "independence." My rebellion against God had not resulted in any overt anti-God activity and my behavior was still commendatory by most church standards. But internally I was going through a fierce struggle concerning the reality of God's existence.

Initially, as I asserted my own independence, I didn't doubt God's existence; rather, I just wished that He didn't exist. There were some things I might like to do that God would disapprove of. In my foolish immaturity I reasoned that if there were no God, I could do whatever I wanted without fear of having to be accountable to higher authority. Now, three years later, I had discovered that "doing my own thing" wasn't all it was cracked up to be.

My interaction with the secular world, especially in college, made me aware that there were smart people who didn't believe in God. I became an amateur agnostic, questioning God's actual existence. Exposed to new ideas and concepts that I had never faced while growing up, I didn't know what to believe. Fortunately, I had matured enough that I actually desired to know truth. I wasn't sophisticated enough to present any kind of intelligible argument for or against God's existence, but I was influenced by authority figures on either side of the question. Certainly my parents, who proclaimed God's reality, were the most powerful authorities for me personally. However, I wasn't eager to know a God who hemmed one in with legalistic dos and don'ts.

14

William James, an eminent Harvard University professor of psychiatry and psychology around the turn of the twentieth century, had significantly influenced my thinking through his classic book, *The Varieties of Religious Experience.* Published in 1902, it is still widely read. Professor James proposed that there were numerous kinds of religious experiences, some having their origin in mental disorder and some in self-hypnosis. But still others were genuinely the result of a "higher power" revealing Himself subliminally. He offered psychological theories for the various experiences. As a result of what I read, I was determined to have my search for truth be as free from invalid external and internal influences as possible.

While waiting for a bus after night class sessions, often I would look up into the vast star-studded Texas sky and think, "Is it possible that all this happened as a result of some sort of cosmic accident? Where did the raw material for the universe originate? Is there really a God who created all this? How can I know who or what to believe?"

GOD REVEALS HIS AWESOME PRESENCE

One night in March, 1948, I was returning to Randolph Field from class particularly engrossed in these sorts of questions. Where could I find an authoritative answer? I knew very well what the Bible said because I had been reared in a home and church where the Bible was the supreme authority. But how could I be certain the Bible was trustworthy?

It was after taps (the bugle call signaling "lights out") that night when I returned to the barracks where I was quartered. I silently climbed into the top bunk where I slept, but this night sleep would not come. My mind was still fully engaged with the questions I had been considering. Suddenly a thought occurred that was astounding in its simplicity but at the same time quite intimidating: "If there really is a God like the Bible describes, He should be able to communicate Himself to me. After all, if He created human beings He should know what makes me tick and how to get through to me." I decided then and there that the only one who could authoritatively reveal God was God Himself. Having reached this conclusion, I crawled out of bed, slipped into

15

my work uniform, and walked the short distance to the Film Strip Preparation Center in search of some privacy.

Unlocking the door and stepping into the large entry area, for a few moments I stood silently, alone in the darkness. The atmosphere and surroundings were just what I desired. There was no music to put me in a spiritually receptive mood, no other person to influence me by his faith or lack of it.

Tentatively I began to speak aloud, "God, I don't know if you exist or if I am just talking into air. But if you are real and you are the God described in the New Testament who really cares about ordinary people like me, I am desperate to know the truth about you. If you have a plan and purpose for my life and can get through to me so that I know you are real, I want to turn my life over to you. Please let me know."

After praying this simple, stumbling prayer I paused, not knowing what might happen, if anything. I certainly had no preconceived ideas of what should or might happen if the God I addressed really existed and responded to my plea. I knew that if He didn't exist or ignored me, I had wasted my time.

As I waited a few moments in the dense darkness that surrounded me, I suddenly became aware of a living Presence in the room. I saw no light, heard no voice, nothing physical touched my body. I was simply acutely conscious of a holy, majestic, awesome, supernatural Presence surrounding me and filling the room. I was shaken to the core and didn't know how to respond. I think I felt like Simon Peter must have felt when he first saw the supernatural power of Jesus displayed in the miraculous catch of fish. Peter exclaimed, "Go away from me, Lord: I am a sinful man!" In my confusion and consternation, I cried out (or maybe it was just a thought unuttered), "God, please don't come on so strong. I don't think I am ready for this!" As soon as these words, or the thought, had been communicated, the hallowed Presence began to gradually and gently withdraw.

Something else had impressed me about this encounter. There had been no sense of condemnation or even disapproval. Lovingly, I had been accepted for what indeed I was a seeker after truth and reality. I was humbled but also elated beyond words. However, my elation was restrained because I knew I had not followed through on my end of the bargain. I had not yet surrendered my life to Him

16

nor did I sense that God was demanding that I do so immediately. There was some unfinished business that must be taken care of before I could surrender my will and destiny to this awesome Being who had revealed a bit of Himself to me.

In the days that followed I thought about the implications of God's breakthrough into my consciousness. No longer could I play the agnostic and say, "If there is a God. . . ." No, now I was forced to say, "Since God is, am I really going to let Him be God of my life?" I had naively thought that if I was sure that the God revealed in the Bible actually existed, it would be easy to follow Him. But for me that did not prove to be true. My own self-will did not surrender so easily. I'm not sure how long I struggled, no more than a week or two, but I at last determined to have it out with God. I was confident I could be honest with Him. My experience in the photo lab convinced me of this. I was determined to lay all my doubts, my fears and reservations before Him and await His response.

MY HOLY SPIRIT BAPTISM EXPERIENCE

Shortly afterward, I attended a Sunday evening service at an Assemblies of God church in San Antonio. At the conclusion of the service all those who had a special spiritual need were invited to come forward and kneel in prayer. With some trepidation I went forward and began to talk to the Lord. I thanked Him for getting through to me so that my doubts were resolved. I reminded Him that as a boy I had desired to serve and please Him and I had gone forward to the altar numerous times to confess my sins and be saved. Every time my conscience had been temporarily relieved and I felt "saved" but soon I was back to my old behavior. I simply did not have the ability to measure up to the standard of holiness the church demanded and I was not interested in repeating another cycle on this religious merry-go-round.

As I prayed I sensed that I was communicating very personally with Jesus Christ. We actually engaged in dialogue, as He was leading me through the process of surrendering my will to Him. He would confront me with an area of my life over which I wanted to retain sovereignty and then He would ask me if I was willing to trust Him with that area. Sometimes it was easy to say

17

"Yes," at other times there was a fierce struggle. For example, when asked if I would be willing to preach the gospel if He called me to that ministry, I resisted. My dad had once counseled me, "Son, never be a preacher if you can do anything else." What Dad meant, of course, was that the ministry was not a profession in the normal sense of the term but, rather, a "calling" placed upon one by God. If one was not sure of his "calling" then he should find another profession. Good advice.

I wasn't yet sure how I wanted to invest my life, but I was sure of two things. One, I did not want to serve in the military after my three-year enlistment was completed. Two, I did not want to be a preacher. But the Lord persisted, "But if I call you to preach, are you willing?" I finally was able to say "Yes," even to this. I could not say "No" to the Lord who had made His love so real to me as we conversed. I would follow Him wherever that took me.

How can I describe the process of the dialogue? If asked if I heard an audible voice, the answer is "No," not if you mean a voice as the result of sound waves striking my eardrums and transmitting them by an intricate physical process through the middle ear on to the cochlea in the inner ear where sensitive hairs trigger nerve signals to the brain. God bypasses all this mechanical process and goes directly to the receiving center in the brain to convey His message. It is not an external shout but an internal whisper, "a still small voice," awesome in its power.

During this whole process I was fully conscious of two different dimensions of reality. I was always aware that I could discontinue the dialogue if I desired. There were times when I was aware of other people near me praying or talking. If I chose, I could focus on that external dimension. But this was never more than a brief distraction. I was captivated by the internal dialogue that demanded my full attention. The Lord led me step by step until I was ready to make a full surrender to His will.

There was just one more issue to be resolved. I told the Lord that I knew I could not serve Him in my own power. I had tried that and failed miserably. I reminded Him of His promise, "You will receive power when the Holy Spirit comes on you."

"Lord, I must have the power of Your Spirit to enable me to live for You." My Pentecostal heritage led me to believe that when one was first baptized in the Holy Spirit, he would speak in an unknown language under the inspiration and direction of the Holy Spirit. I had no idea how the Holy Spirit would do this but I was willing for Him to speak through me if He chose. I had been taught that since the tongue was the most unruly organ of the body, when it was surrendered to the Holy Spirit it signified a total surrender to God.

I knew that Jesus Himself was the one who baptized believers in the Holy Spirit, so I began to focus all my attention and worship on Jesus. I thanked Him for suffering on the cross on my behalf and paying the penalty for my sins.

With arms raised in adoration and surrender, I thanked Jesus again and again for His love and forgiveness. I groped for words to express more completely my gratitude and joy for all He was doing in my life. In an instant I was aware that the Holy Spirit wanted to help me give expression to what I was feeling. But the Spirit never arbitrarily took control. I knew that I had the option of retaining control of my speech or surrendering to His guidance.

In joy and trust I said "Yes" to the Spirit of God and immediately I began to speak clearly in a language that was completely foreign to me. As I was borne along by the Spirit, I listened to myself in amazement. The enunciation was crystal clear and all the elements of a spoken language were evident. There were rising and falling inflections, indicating statements and questions.

There were some statements soft and matter-of-fact, some more passionate and intense. It was like a speech or perhaps a sermon in which I was both speaker and listener. I had a wonderful sense of God's presence but had no idea what was being said. (This phenomenon must have continued for twenty minutes or so, long enough for a good sermon, as I learned many years later at Princeton Seminary.)

My initial commitment to Jesus Christ was complete and I sensed a glorious new freedom. My future was now in the hands of God Himself. I was overwhelmed with the wonder of it all and the internal turmoil that had been raging was now replaced by a marvelous peace.

CHAPTER 2

AN ARGUMENT FOR SUPERNATURAL EVENTS

Atheists and materialists of all sorts will discount my experience with God and attempt to explain it away with some sort of naturalistic scientific or psychological explanation.

According to Professor Norman Geisler much of their philosophy is based on some form of Benedict Spinoza's argument against supernatural events. This Jewish philosopher (1632-1677), arguing from Newton's ideas of natural law, declared, *"Nothing then, comes to pass in nature in contravention to her universal laws, nay, nothing does not agree with them and follow from them, for . . . she keeps a fixed and immutable order."* He goes on to say, *"A miracle, whether in contravention to, or beyond, nature, is a mere absurdity. . . . We may, then, be absolutely certain that every event which is truly described in Scripture necessarily happened, like everything else, according to natural laws."* (Truth Journal "Miracles and Modern Scientific Thought, Prof. Norman Geisler: www.leaderu.com/truth/1truth19.html)

Geisler summarizes Spinoza's argument this way:

1. *"Miracles are violation of natural laws."*
2. *"Natural laws are immutable."*
3. *"It is impossible for immutable laws to be violated."*
4. *"Therefore, miracles are impossible."* (Ibid.)

By definition, a miracle is a unique event that cannot be proved by repetition. Should a believer agree that his "miracle" cannot be repeated for observation, then the anti-supernaturalist would classify it as a statistical improbability (like a hole-in-one) or a fluke. If a theist insists that, despite no repeatable evidence, he accepts by faith alone that a miracle has taken place, then he has entered the quagmire of subjectivism. Subjective faith is never a valid substitute for truth. A child may believe fervently in Santa Claus but her faith is no substitute for reality, despite all the presents "Santa brought" lying under the Christmas tree.

Many philosophers and scientists from the time of Spinoza have argued that miracles and a commitment to modern scientific methodology are incompatible. Professor Geisler has presented an excellent refutation of the arguments for this position. He examines the classic positions of Spinoza, Hume and on down to men like Alastair McKinnon and Carl Sagan of modern times. These assert there can be no scientific proof of a miracle since only events that are demonstrated to be uniformly repeatable can be scientifically affirmed.

Geisler contends that to fall back on faith alone without any repeatable evidence makes it impossible to refute the skeptic. If I firmly believe that Mars is inhabited by an alien race of space creatures, who is to say I am wrong if faith instead of truth is the basis for reality? Professor Geisler then presents a very cogent, carefully reasoned argument, demonstrating that theists do not have to surrender the repeatable evidence criteria.

The beauty of Professor Geisler's effort is that he turns the skeptic's fundamental principle of repeatability around to undermine some of their most sacred cows. Many naturalistic scientists accept the "big bang" theory as a viable explanation for the origin of the universe. However, it is a non-repeatable event and therefore cannot be proven. It must be accepted on faith and not on the basis of science. The professor then shrewdly presents two other unique events for which naturalistic scientists claim to have a scientific basis: the spontaneous generation of life on earth and the macro-evolution of species, both which occurred only once.

To escape the charge of basic theories themselves being unscientific, the materialists introduced another principle: past singular events can be understood in the light of present similar regular recurring events. For example, the late astronomer Carl Sagan, an outspoken foe of supernaturalism, ardently believed that even one message received from outer space would prove the existence of intelligent extraterrestrial beings. Why? Because countless messages received in space have all originated from intelligent beings. So the materialistic scientists introduced this principle: All single events must be understood in the light of similar regular ongoing events. But on the basis of this very principle, the objection to supernaturalists for their belief in unique miraculous events is undermined. If Sagan can be sure there is an intelligent source for a unique event based on repeated experiences of similar events, then theists can confidently assert there is an intelligent Source for the origin of life for the same reason.

To quote Professor Geisler: *"All observational evidence indicates that the nonliving never produces the living. Pasteur's experiments disproved spontaneous generation long ago. There is a uniform and universally available experience as a basis for this conclusion, and there are no verified exceptions. Hence, the argument against spontaneous generation is as firmly scientific as any such arguments can be."* (Ibid.)

In other words, the evolutionist's insistence that life began from nonlife has no regular antecedents and can only be accepted by faith. It cannot be expounded as fact.

The sad truth is that many evolutionists have such a blind faith commitment to their materialistic world view that they are not open to opposing evidence. Dr. Craig Keener, author of a monumental new book entitled *Miracles*, quotes this pertinent observation from Charles Talbert: *"The materialistic worldview . . . dictates that the world was and is ruled by iron physical laws that not even God could or can bend."* Keener points out the obvious: *"This, however, is a worldview and not an argument. . . . One philosopher warns that those who dismiss miracles yet are unwilling to offer solid arguments need to 'admit that they have a faith commitment which precludes the possibility of miracles.'"* (Craig Keener, *Miracles*, p. 100-101).

On the other hand, the miracle of life generated by an intelligent Creator is supported by multiplied examples of life producing life. The Christian does not have to retreat into subjective experience as his sole basis for believing in supernatural events. An infinitely intelligent and powerful Creator can reveal himself to intelligent creatures through supernatural means as well natural. I had not the slightest doubt that God had revealed Himself to me. He had accommodated himself to my limitations. Through the ministry of the Holy Spirit I clearly recognized Him as the self-revealing God of Scripture who came among us in the person of Jesus Christ.

No wonder anti-supernaturalists desperately try to undermine belief that God exists. If there is indeed an omnipotent, omniscient Creator then He can interpose His creativity wherever and whenever He chooses. Thus, the supernatural can override the natural when the Creator so wills. All the big guns of scientism (the religion spawned by those who believe science is supreme) are aimed at destroying the credibility of those scientists who advance evidence that supports the idea of intelligent design in the very structure of the universe.

In recent years one well-informed Christian author has turned the tables on the ardent atheists who are attempting to undermine belief in God in general and in Christianity in particular. The author is Dinesh D'Souza and the book is *What's So Great About Chrisitanity.* Renowned scholar and author Stanley Fish has this to say about the book: "The great merit of this book is that it concedes nothing. Rather than engaging in the usual defensive ploys, D'Souza meets every anti-God argument head on and defeats it on its own terms. He subjects atheism and scientific materialism to sustained rigorous interrogation and shows that their claims are empty and incoherent. Infinitely more sophisticated than the rants produced by Richard Dawkins, Sam Harris, and Christopher Hitchens. *What's So Great About Christianity* leaves those atheist books in the dust." (Testimonial inside cover)

I have read this book twice and have gained fresh insights each time. For example, I had long been perplexed by the Genesis creation account which records light created on day one (Genesis 1:3) but the sun is not created until day four (Genesis 1:14-19). D'Souza explains, "The Big Bang resolves one of the apparent contradictions in the book of Genesis. For more than two centuries, critics of the Bible have pointed out that in the beginning—on the first day—God created light. Then on the fourth day God separated the night from the day. The problem is pointed out by philosopher Leo Strauss: 'Light is presented as preceding the sun. . . .' The writer of Genesis seemed to have made an obvious mistake.

"But it turns out there is no mistake. The universe was created in a burst of light fifteen billion years ago. Our sun and our planet came into existence billions of years later. So light did indeed precede the sun. The first reference to light in Genesis can be seen to refer to the Big Bang itself . . . The Genesis enigma is solved and its account of creation is vindicated not as some vague parable but as a strikingly accurate account of how the universe came to be." (Dinesh D'Souza, *What's So Great about Christianity, pp. 125-26)*

The scientific world now, by and large, accepts the reality introduced by the Big Bang theory. Astronomer Martin Rees acknowledges "that numerous lines of evidence have now converged that have discredited the steady state theory and confirmed the Big Bang theory." (Martin Rees, *Just Six Numbers, The Deep Forces That Shape the Universe* New York: Basic Books, 2000, p. 11) D'Souza goes on to inflict the coup de grace to the atheistic taunts. "Now is the time to supply the 'missing link' and show that the universe did have a creator. The proof is extremely simple. Everything that begins to exist has a cause. The universe began to exist. Therefore, the universe has a cause. That cause we call God." (Ibid. p.127)

THE REBELLIOUS EVOLUTIONIST EGO

Have you ever asked yourself, as I have, why scientists promoting materialistic scientism (many do not) go to such extremes to protect their theory from valid scientific investigation? I have come to the conclusion there are two primary reasons. One is spiritual, the other egotistical.

The spiritual reason is the same one I experienced when I wanted to do my thing without interference from God. Human beings are in rebellion against their Creator. However one interprets what took place in Eden, it is clear that man wanted to hide from God's presence after rebelling. Their current hiding place is among the trees in the garden of materialistic scientism. To have their nakedness revealed by scientists that do not buy into their theology is very threatening and disconcerting. I say "theology" because evolution is admittedly a religion, as some of its chief advocates acknowledge.

Michael Ruse, professor of history and philosophy and author of books defending Darwinism, including *Taking Darwin Seriously*, readily admits that evolution is religious: "Evolution is

24

promoted by practitioners as more than mere science. Evolution is promulgated as an ideology, a secular religion—a full-fledged alternative to Christianity, with meaning and morality. I am an ardent evolutionist and an ex-Christian, but I must admit to this one complaint, the literalist (i.e. creationists) are absolutely right. "Evolution is a religion. This was true of evolution in the beginning and it is true of evolution still today." (*National Post,* May 13, 2000, p. E-3)

Richard Lewontin, an evolutionary biologist states: "It is not that the methods and institutions of science somehow compel us to accept a material explanation of the phenomenal world, but on the contrary, that we are forced by our a priori adherence to material causes to create an apparatus of investigation and a set of concepts that produce material explanations, no matter how counter-intuitive, no matter how mystifying to the uninitiated. Moreover, that materialism is an absolute, for we cannot allow a Divine Foot in the door." (Quoted by Henry Morris in *Evolution is religion – Not Science,* www.icr.org/articles/view/455/266)

Egoism is another reason that evolutionists suppress anything or anyone that might threaten their citadel. Their professional reputations will be destroyed if intelligent design takes root in academia. That must not happen even if it demands destroying careers of colleagues who threaten their sacred materialism.

THE EVOLUTIONIST / SADDUCEE PARALLEL

The materialists of Jesus' day were the Sadducees, who denied the supernatural. They did not believe in a resurrection nor in angels and demons. They adhered to the Greek philosophy of Epicurus, believing the soul ceased to exist after death, thus there was no future judgment, no punishment, no rewards. They lived only for the present and sought power and pleasure at whatever cost.

Sadduceeism lives on in the religion of secular evolutionism. It has invaded our school campuses in the cleverly disguised role of science. Human beings are just cosmic accidents with no intrinsic worth. Are we surprised that youth turn to booze, drugs and illicit sex? This is but the modern equivalent of the ancient Sadducees' materialistic philosophy, "Eat, drink and make merry for tomorrow we die." If you believe you have no future beyond the grave, no intrinsic value, no eternal destiny, what does it matter if you abuse yourself or others? Just get as much pleasure as possible, avoid as much pain as you can, because life on earth is a one-way, dead-end street, and there are no U-turns.

JESUS' CLAIMS AUTHENTICATED
BY THE SUPERNATURAL

Imagine the consternation of the Sadducees when Jesus appeared claiming to be the Son of God and the Messiah promised by the prophets. His claims might have been discounted as the ravings of a mad man or a pernicious deceiver except they were authenticated by miracles. Could this be possible? Yes!

Witness after witness proclaimed that Jesus performed supernatural signs and wonders. At His command, the blind had sight restored, lepers were cleansed, the diseased healed, the lame walked, even the dead were restored to life. The very philosophical foundation of the Sadducees was being destroyed, miracle by miracle. Jesus audaciously challenged them to let the miracles speak for Him if they did not believe His words.

The Sadducees' influence was shattered. They were desperate to destroy Jesus, so desperate that they entered into a pact with the Pharisees, their historical enemies. They pledged to work together to end the life of Jesus of Nazareth. Their connivance, with the help of a weak-willed Roman governor, resulted in Jesus' crucifixion. But this was the God-ordained prelude to the greatest miracle of all. The resurrection of Jesus followed on the third day after His crucifixion. This was the unique supernatural act that authenticated every claim of Jesus. It was witnessed by hundreds of people, transformed fearful followers into bold proclaimers of the gospel, and launched Christianity throughout the Roman Empire and beyond.

The first disciples were creatures of their own culture just as we are creatures of ours. They anticipated that the Messiah, the "Son of David," would be a political conqueror just as His forefather had been. They were convinced that Jesus would use His supernatural power to overthrow Rome and establish the messianic kingdom foretold by the prophets.

When the disciples inquired as to the exact time they could

expect to see His kingdom inaugurated, they received an unexpected reply. "Dates and times are not your business. They are in my Father's hands. I want you to go back to Jerusalem and await the coming of the Holy Spirit which I promised to send. When He comes upon you, you shall receive power to be my witnesses wherever I send you." After saying this, Jesus ascended bodily out of their sight.

THE HOLY SPIRIT'S SUPERNATURAL DESCENT

The disciples returned to Jerusalem as ordered. When the feast of Pentecost arrived, the Holy Spirit flooded the room where the disciples waited. The Spirit's coming was accompanied by supernatural phenomena . . . the sound of rushing wind, the sight of fiery flames resting on all present, and unknown languages being spoken by all the disciples. It was the speaking of languages that caught the attention of crowds of tourists outside the house who had come from all over the Roman Empire to celebrate Pentecost. The discovery of their native languages being spoken by uneducated Galileans created a huge stir.

Their amazement and curiosity gave the apostle Peter an opportunity to explain what was happening. While he had their undivided attention, he proceeded to proclaim Jesus as the Messiah who had come but had been rejected, crucified, buried and then raised from the dead. The many miracles performed by Jesus when He was on earth, His resurrection, ascension and now the miracles attending the outpouring of the Holy Spirit all were referenced by Peter as proving Jesus was both Lord and Messiah. Peter exhorted the assembled multitude to repent and be baptized in the name of Jesus Christ, and then they too would receive the gift of the Holy Spirit. Three thousand responded and the church was born.

MIRACLES AND THE EARLY CHURCH

Miracles figured largely in the birth of the church. The variety and dramatic impact of miracles performed through the power of the Holy Spirit continued to play a significant role in the growth of the church. Acts 5 is pulsating with excitement and wonder:

"The apostles performed many miraculous signs and wonders

among the people. . . . More and more men and women believed in the Lord and were added to their number. . . . Crowds gathered also from the towns around Jerusalem, bringing their sick and those tormented by evil spirits, and all of them were healed." (vv. 12-16)

But it was not only the apostles that were empowered by the Spirit to bring miraculous deliverance to the sick and oppressed. Acts 6 records the account of a believer named Stephen: "Now Stephen, a man full of God's grace and power, did great wonders and miraculous signs among the people." (v. 8)

Another believer named Philip was gifted as an evangelist; we read about his evangelistic endeavors in Samaria: "When the crowds heard Philip and saw the miraculous signs he did, they all paid close attention to what he said." (Acts 8:6)

The point I wish to make is that if one accepts the historical testimony of the New Testament, he can't deny that supernatural miracles contributed significantly to the advancement of the early church. The miracles helped authenticate the truth of the gospel; they motivated honest seekers of truth to examine the claims of Christianity. The miraculous was not the foundation of the church. Truth was its foundation and Jesus Christ was truth personified.

Miracles, however, were objective facts that made the supernatural claims of Jesus Christ credible. Jesus Himself used this very argument against His violent critics: "Why then do you accuse me of blasphemy because I said, 'I am God's Son'? Do not believe me unless I do what my Father does. But if I do it, even though you do not believe me, believe the evidence of the miracles, that you may know and understand that the Father is in me, and I in the Father" (John 10:36-38).

Jesus even appealed to miracles to bolster faith in His disciples just in case they doubted His words. Jesus is engaged in dialogue with His disciples following the Passover meal in the Upper Room. Philip has asked Him to show them the Father and "then they will be satisfied." Jesus responds, "Believe me when I say that I am in the Father and the Father is in me; or at least believe on the evidence of the miracles themselves." (John 14:11) Numerous times in the book of Acts the miracles performed through the disciples were used to bolster the messianic claims of Jesus. Supernatural events wrought by the power of the Holy Spirit continue today and still establish the truth of Jesus Christ around the world.

CHAPTER 3

LESSONS TO BE LEARNED FROM MONTANISM

Historically, the church has gone through periods of declension and spiritual apathy. The personal relationship with Jesus Christ is replaced by legalistic religious requirements, worldly entertainment or some other substitute for fellowship with our Lord. The Holy Spirit is active in those periods to draw Christians back to an intimate relationship with God. One of the earliest and best known attempts to renew spiritual life in the church is known as Montanism. The church had lost much of her intense spiritual fervor by mid second century. This challenged a Christian by the name of Montanus to initiate reform. In his classic *History of the Christian Church,* Philip Schaff describes the reform movement this way: "*All the ascetic, rigoristic, and chiliastic elements of the ancient church combined in Montanism. They there asserted a claim to universal validity, which the Catholic Church was compelled, for her own interest, to reject, since she left the effort after extraordinary holiness to the comparatively small circle of ascetics and priests, and sought to lighten Christianity rather than add to its weight, for the great mass of its professors.... Montanism was not, originally, a departure from the faith, but a morbid overstraining of the practical morality and discipline of the early church. It was an excessive supernaturalism and Puritanism against Gnostic rationalism and Catholic laxity. It is the first example of an earnest and well-meaning, but gloomy and fanatical, hyper-Christianity, which, like all hyper-spiritualism, is apt to end in the flesh.*" *(Phillip Schaff, History of the Christian church, Vol. II, p. 417)*

Montanism has been likened to modern Pentecostalism. There are some interesting parallels but also significant differences. I am interested in this subject because I think Pentecostal/Charismatic believers can learn important lessons from what transpired in the church over eighteen hundred years ago.

While doing research on this subject, I was surprised to find that a prominent Pentecostal scholar and teacher had come to the same conclusion. Donald Gee wrote in the December, 1928, issue

30

of Redemption Tidings an article entitled "Montanism."

It begins: *"The study of the reasons for failure and mistakes is almost invariably the stepping-stone to ultimate victory and success. The church can learn many lessons from the various errors in doctrine and practice that have flourished for a time during her history, even while at the same time she can praise God for the wonderful way He has preserved His truth through all the welter of centuries of human imperfection. We are persuaded that a brief study of the Montanist heresy of the second century is likely to prove very profitable just now. Indeed, we seem almost driven to it when certain opponents of the present gracious Latter Rain Outpouring of the Holy Spirit are plainly stating that the Pentecostal movement is only a revival of Montanism."* (Donald Gee, "Montantism" in Redemption Tidings, December, 1928)

MONTANISM AND PENTECOSTAL SIMILARITIES

First, look at the parallels between Montanism and the Pentecostal movement.

• **The driving motivation for Montanus was reformation of the church through restoration of the gifts bestowed by the Holy Spirit.**

Montanism spread because there was a genuine hunger for a return to primitive Christianity among believers. It was not heretical in the beginning. Schaff observes, *"In doctrine, Monatanism agreed in all essential points with the Catholic Church, and held very firmly to the traditional rule of faith."*

They initially accepted the authority of the Old and New Testament Scriptures and were orthodox Trinitarians. Montanus introduced renewed emphasis upon the activity of the Holy Spirit in the body of Christ and soon the gifts of the Spirit were evident.

Likewise, the Assemblies of God was organized by men and women who had experienced an outpouring of the Holy Spirit with miraculous signs and spiritual gifts in evidence. They desired this experience for all Christians.

• **The Montanists asserted the universal priesthood of all Christians, including women.**

This was in sharp contrast to the special class of male priests sanctioned by the Catholic Church. This seems to be a genuine

31

effort to replace a male-dominated hierarchy with Paul's ideal, "There is neither Jew nor Greek, slave nor free, male nor female, for you are all one in Christ Jesus." (Galatians 3:28) Montanus, in fact, was accompanied by two female prophetesses, Priscilla and Maximilla. There is some historical indication that they may have been more influential in the movement than Montanus himself. From the beginning women likewise figured prominently in the Pentecostal movement. They were ordained as evangelists, missionaries and, to a lesser degree, pastors. They continue to minister effectively in many arenas of service.

• **The Montanists were ardent and militant millennialists. They anticipated the imminent return of Jesus to establish His thousand-year kingdom upon earth. This view caused them to look with contempt upon the social order of this world since it was soon passing away.**

Philip Schaff, the historian, describes their view as follows: *"The Montanists were the warmest millenarians in the ancient church, and held fast to the speedy return of Christ in Glory. . . . In praying, 'Thy kingdom come,' they prayed for the end of the world. They lived under a vivid impression of the great final catastrophe, and looked therefore with contempt upon the present order of things, and directed all their desires to the second advent of Christ."* (Ibid. Schaff)

Pentecostals believe and proclaim the imminent return of Jesus to catch away true believers. I can well remember the fervor with which this doctrine was preached. As a child I lived in fear of Jesus coming and leaving me behind. A train whistle, a police siren, or some other unexpected loud sound instantly aroused the question in my childish mind, "Is that the last trumpet?"

Within the Assemblies of God this emphasis produced two dissimilar responses. On the one hand, it provided tremendous motivation for missionary activity so as to get the gospel out before the Lord's return. On the other hand, it motivated some to withdraw from the world and concentrate on personal holiness. Overall, outreach won out over halo polishing.

• **In their effort to counter the loose morals prevalent in the Catholic Church, the Montanists fell into severe asceticism and legalism.**

It denied women all ornamental clothing and declared all art to be incompatible with Christian holiness. Pentecostal believers did not go to this extreme but asceticism and legalism were prevalent in most churches when I was growing up.

• **The Montanists rejected all clergy. They believed the office of Prophet had been restored and all teaching was relegated to the prophets. They taught that any believer could become a prophet.**

This teaching ran counter to the teaching of the church which accepted clergy (pastors, teachers, evangelists etc.) as necessary for operation of the church. Apparently, as long as Montanus lived, the prophetic teachings were subjected to the test of adhering to scripture. Later, zealous prophets claiming to speak for God, refused the biblical test and their prophecies usurped scripture. This led to the condemnation of Montanism by the bishop of Rome. . The movement began to die in the third century but pockets persisted into the eighth century.

MONTANISTIC AND PENTECOSTAL DIFFERENCES

Consider now where Montanism has nothing in common with the Pentecostal movement, particularly the Assemblies of God.

The prophecies of Montanus and other prophets were eventually seen as superseding the prophecies of the inspired apostles.

Some of the early leaders in the formative stages of The Assemblies of God were guilty of promoting prophetic utterances as more valid than scripture. This was particularly true of the group that denied the Trinity (Jesus only). Some of the those initially involved in forming the Assemblies of God were so impressed by the exuberance of speaking in tongues exhibited by "Jesus Only" adherents that they changed sides. Once experience is given ascendancy over the divine revelation of scripture then theology is on a slippery slope of subjectivism.

Donald Gee definitively supports this. I quote again from his article in Redemption Tidings on Montanism: *"What caused Montanism to go so grievously astray? We unhesitatingly suggest that the answer must be: the undue emphasis and authority placed upon 'prophetic' utterances and visions. These quickly became the one outstanding feature of the whole movement....We believe the present office of the Holy Spirit is not to add to the body of written revelation, but to unfold the treasures of the Divine Revelation contained within the Sacred Scriptures."* (Ibid, Gee)

Gee then goes on to add this pertinent warning: *"Away down at the root of the error of Montanism, and every similar movement that has or does magnify prophetical utterances up to an equal level with the Scriptures, is a mistaken idea of the real nature of spiritual gifts. This idea clothes utterances through spiritual gifts with an authority and importance which they do not possess. The mistake may be held in all sincerity, but it can be nonetheless mischievous. It can be held theoretically by those who repudiate any practical experience of these things, and can lead them as far astray in their doctrine as it will others in their practice."* (Ibid.)

Donald Gee wrote more than eighty years ago in the early days of the Pentecostal revival. Despite Gee's warning, Pentecostals have elevated speaking in tongues to a place similar to the gift of prophecy in early Montanism. The supremecy of scripture was given lip service in most Pentecostal groups. Unfortunately, scripture did not prevail but experience was given the primacy. My research shows that founders of the Assemblies of God vigorously discouraged dissenting voices in the founding General Council (1914) to be raised against the dogma of evidential tongues. The decision was made by a coterie so enamored with speaking in tongues (a valid spiritual gift) that they would not permit a careful exegetical study of pertinent scriptures to determine the purpose of tongues. This despite the fact that scripture clearly declares why tongues accompanied the outpouting of the Spirit at Pentecost. And it wasn't to signify a valid Spirit baptism.

Another error propounded by Montanists but rejected by the ancient church, and certainly by Pentecostals today, is that Christians who fall from grace cannot be restored. The Assemblies of God has always taught that grace trumps judgment and that true repentance leads to restoration.

Montanism's emphasis upon asceticism and legalistic observances exceeded anything advocated by Pentecostals. Marriages were discouraged and second marriages were forbidden as adulterous. It courted martyrdom and forbade concealment or flight in order to escape persecution.

The evidence seems to support church historian Philip Schaff's conclusion that Montanism began as a reform movement with genuine supernatural manifestations of spiritual gifts. This counters the assertion that manifestation of the gifts ceased with the apostles. It was only as the Montanist prophets began to promote their prophecies as more authoritative than that of the original apostles that excesses and errors arose. This same grievous error was evident among Pentecostals one hundred years ago. The group that denied the Trinity claimed their doctrine must be true because their adherents spoke in tongues more than all others. Some who had been part of the group that was forming the Assemblies of God were so swayed by this teaching they left and joined the "Jesus Only" segment of Pentecostalism.

Montanism began as a valid movement to restore spiritual power to a weak church. It failed in its mission because it did not continually subject its doctrine and experiences to the scrutiny and discipline of Scripture. Our examination of Montanism then serves two purposes.

1. **It reveals that the operation of spiritual gifts continued beyond the apostolic age.** Of course, there are other historical documents that confirm miracles and gifts of the Spirit were never entirely lost to the church. Augustine (354-430 A.D.), while initially believing miracles had ceased, in the later years of his life saw evidence that convinced him he was wrong. In Book 22, chapter 8 of *The City of God*, he records miracles which he had personally seen or which had been reported by reliable witnesses. Venerable Bede's Ecclesiastical History of the English People, written in early eighth century, is chock full of accounts of miracles. We can put to rest the assertion that miracles and gifts of the Spirit died with the apostles.

2. **It demonstrates how error can develop among the best intentioned believers if subjective spiritual experiences are not governed by Scripture.** The Assemblies of God asserts that spiritual experiences must be evaluated in accordance with Scripture. Unfortunately, they fail to do this with their doctrine of tongues as required evidence of Spirit baptism. Instead they attempt to use an isolated proof text upon which to base a major doctrine and disregard the totality of contextual exegesis.

CHAPTER 4

ARE SPIRITUAL GIFTS FOR
THE CHURCH TODAY?

Are the supernatural gifts of the Holy Spirit meant to be in operation in the church today?

When I was admitted to the Denver Conservative Baptist Seminary (now Denver Seminary) in 1954, I was the only Pentecostal in the student body. I was soon exposed to the Baptist theology of cessationism, the teaching that the supernatural gifts employed by Christ and the apostles—such as gifts of healing, tongues and interpretations, miracles—ended when the apostles all died.

THE CESSATIONIST TRADITION

I knew Baptists were reputed to lay great store upon the authority of Scripture. I was an open-minded student eagerly seeking truth and I sought scriptural proof for the cessationist position from the New Testament and my theology professors.

The best I could get was 1 Corinthians 13:8-10: "Love never fails. But where there are prophecies, they will cease; where there are tongues, they will be stilled; where there is knowledge, it will pass away. For we know in part and we prophesy in part, but when perfection comes, the imperfect disappears."

Even if that little phrase "where there is knowledge" hadn't been included in the things that pass away, this proof text still falls flat on its face. With that phrase included, to interpret it as proving spiritual gifts stopped when the apostles died is sheer fabrication to support a position imposed by tradition, not Scripture.

John MacArthur, Jr. is a leading advocate of this cessationist tradition. He comments on this passage: *"In 1 Corinthians 13:8 Paul made an interesting, almost startling, statement: 'Love never fails; but if there are gifts of prophecy, they will be done away; if there are tongues, they will cease; if there is knowledge, it will be done away.' In the expression 'love never fails,' the Greek word translated 'fails' means 'to decay' or 'to be abolished'. . .*

36

Tongues, however, 'will cease.' The Greek verb used in 1 Corinthians 13:8 'pauo' means to 'cease permanently.' It implies that when tongues ceased, they would never start up again." (John MacArthur, Jr. *Charismatic Chaos*, pp. 230-31)

Before I continue with MacArthur's quote, let me say that his Greek exegesis is all wrong. *Pauo* does not mean to "cease permanently." It means to finish, cease or to refrain. (It is the same root word as the English word "pause.") This verb is used twelve times in the New Testament, first in Luke 5:4 where Jesus is teaching from a boat occupied by Simon Peter and other fishermen. Luke records, "When he had finished (ceased, *pauo*) speaking, he said to Simon..." Did Jesus cease speaking permanently? What a travesty of exegesis MacArthur has fallen into.

Another typical episode that demonstrates MacArthur's error is found in Luke 11:1. Jesus is praying and Luke records, "When he finished (pauo). . . ." Did Jesus cease praying permanently? How absurd. I could continue giving further examples from the New Testament but it would be needless repetition. It is evident that MacArthur has completely misinterpreted this passage.

Although the Greek verb doesn't demand it, it is true that tongues will cease, just as gifts of prophecy and knowledge will pass away. But that will only happen when "perfection comes, the imperfect disappears." And when does perfection come? When we see our Lord face to face.

The eminent theologian and Greek scholar, R. C. H. Lenski, comments on the 1 Corinthians 13 passage: *"Paul is speaking regarding the consummation when Christ shall return in glory, when the kingdom of grace shall merge into the kingdom of glory. Then all need of prophets will cease and also all need of the revelations which they have made to us here below and of the instructions and the admonition which they gave us, for heaven itself will reveal all its mysteries to us directly. Tongues and languages such as we know at present shall no longer be needed, for all of us shall understand and speak the perfect language of heaven. Study, reasoning, and learning will no longer be needed, for instead of this gift which was granted to only a few and on which many depend, the new earth shall be filled with the heavenly knowledge of the glory of the Lord as the waters cover the sea."*

37

(R.C.H. Lenski, The Interpretation of 1st and 2nd Corinthians, pp 563-64)

MacArthur then goes on to say: *"Here is the problem this passage poses for the contemporary charismatic movement; if tongues were supposed to cease, has that already happened, or is it yet future? Charismatic brothers in Christ insist that none of the gifts have ceased yet, so the cessation of tongues is yet future. Most noncharismatics insist that tongues have already ceased, passing away with the apostolic age. Who is right?"* (Ibid. p. 231)

MacArthur insists that the cessationists are right. But he has absolutely no scriptural basis for his theory. The passage above which he tries to twist into his outmoded tradition just won't fit. I grant my brother many of the abuses he associates with tongues and charismatics. I deplore them probably more than he does. But I am working on a solution, not a dismissal of the reality of the gifts.

MacArthur's argument for cessationism could never gain a hearing among Evangelicals except in the West (USA, Canada, Europe). Miracles reminiscent of the book of Acts are exploding among Evangelicals in Asia, Africa, and S. America. In some areas such as Korea this has been going on for years. There is an intriguing story of indigenous Korean Presbyterians and the resident North American missionaries. The Western Presbyterian missionaries imported their cessation doctrine to the Korean church. A significant Korean revival broke out around the turn of the twentieth century.

Kil Sun Ju, a revival leader and later a martyr during foreign occupation, contended that miracles had not ceased. Ik Doo Kim, most popular Korean Protestant preacher, reported numerous healings and other signs during his ministry. The reports included the healing of blindness, paralysis, hemophilia, speech restored to mutes and lame walking. A Commission was assigned to evaluate the miracle claims. The Commission astounded the missionaries by confirming that genuine miracles had occurred. "In 1923 the Korean Presbyterian Church officially abandoned the doctrine that miracles had ceased, widely held at that time by North American Presbyterians." (*Miracles* by Dr. Craig Keener, p. 291)

HAVE SPIRITUAL GIFTS CEASED?

Another argument advanced by cessationists affirmed that spiritual gifts had not been seen in the church since apostolic times. Ipso facto, the Holy Spirit no longer gifts Christians as He did in apostolic days. Up until the beginning of the twentieth century, this was partially true but never completely. A few of the church fathers made reference to the gifts, particularly Augustine. And there were the Montanists whom the Western church father, Tertullian, clearly endorsed until their excesses transgressed Scripture. But, I might add, an argument from silence doesn't really prove anything one way or the other.

THE AZUSA STREET REVIVAL

The cessationist argument took on a new challenger just over a hundred years ago. In 1906 on Azusa Street in Los Angeles, California, a dramatic revival of the gifts of the Spirit was displayed before the world. God in his wisdom and sovereignty anointed William Seymour, a black pastor who was blind in one eye, as leader of this Pentecostal outpouring. Most were blue-collar, working-class with a smattering of well-educated, white-collar types. The common denominator that brought them to a run-down mission church on Azusa Street was a hunger for a demonstration of the reality of God's power. Word had spread that God was doing something powerful, if very unusual, and the curious flocked to observe what was happening.

"By mid-May, 1906, anywhere from 300 to 1500 people would attempt to fit into the building. Since horses had very recently been the residents of the building, flies constantly bothered the attendees. People from a great diversity of backgrounds came together to worship: men, women, children, black, white, Hispanic, Asian, rich, poor, illiterate, and educated. People of all ages flocked to Los Angeles with both skepticism and a desire to participate. The intermingling of races and the group's encouragement of women in leadership is remarkable, as 1906 was the height of the 'Jim Crow' era of racial segregation and fourteen years prior to women receiving suffrage in the United States." (www.wikipedia.org/Azusa Street Revival)

An observer described a typical service this way: *"No instruments of music are used. None are needed. No choir—the angels have been heard by some in the Spirit. No collections are taken. No bills have been posted to advertise the meetings. No church organization is back of it. All who are in touch with God realize as soon as they enter the meetings that the Holy Ghost is the leader."* (Ibid.)

Another report said: *"Proud, well-dressed preachers came to 'investigate.' Soon their high looks were replaced with wonder, then conviction comes, and very often you will find them in a short time wallowing on the dirty floor, asking God to forgive them and make them as little children."* (Ibid.)

A reporter for *The Los Angeles Times* wrote a scathing report: *"Meetings are held in a tumble-down shack on Azusa Street, and the devotees of the weird doctrine practice the most fanatical rites, preach the wildest theories and work themselves into a state of mad excitement in their peculiar zeal. Colored people and a sprinkling of whites compose the congregation, and night is made hideous in the neighborhood by the howlings of the worshippers, who spend hours swaying back and forth in a nerve-racking attitude of prayer and supplication. They claim to have the 'gift of tongues' and be able to understand the babel (sic)."*

The scriptural gifts of the Spirit were being exercised and many miracles were widely reported. These included remarkable healings and speaking in languages not understood by the speaker but understood by visiting foreigners. Participants included clergy and laymen from a variety of denominations. In addition to different groups from the Holiness movement, there were Baptists, Mennonites, Presbyterians, and Quakers. They were drawn together by a mutual hunger for more than thoughtful sermons and good works that characterized the church of the day. They desired the supernatural power of the Holy Spirit that energized the apostolic church to again be evident in the church. God heard their cry and the Azusa Street revival resulted.

SOCIETY RESPONDS TO THE AZUSA STREET REVIVAL

What was society's response to all this? The secular world responded much as reported in The Los Angeles Times—it was all the result of religious fanaticism and should not be taken seriously. The fact that it was led by a one-eyed black pastor and attended largely by blacks didn't elevate it in the eyes of the press. But it drew large crowds and created great interest, so the press covered it and in the process sold more papers and made more money.

It takes the longer look of history to capture the real significance of Azusa Street. Pentecostal scholar Dr. Allan Anderson of Selley Oak Colleges in Birmingham, England, has said it well:

"The impetus which generated the international Pentecostal movement originated in a black church in Azusa Street, Los Angeles, where the Pentecostal emphasis of 'Spirit baptism' was propagated by William Seymour, son of African slaves. Lovett points out that al-though Azusa Street was a model of interracial harmony, it was a black church to which whites came, led by the unpretentious Seymour who had earlier endured the ignominy of sitting outside the door of white Pentecostal leader Charles Parham's Bible school in Houston.

"The Azusa Street revival continued for three years without interruption, and became the center to which people flocked, 'received the Spirit,' and from which the message of 'Pentecost' was carried all over the world, reaching fifty nations within two years. During North America's worst racial period, people of all races and social backgrounds 'achieved a new sense of dignity and community in fully integrated Pentecostal services.'" (Dr. Allan Anderson, *African Pentecostal Churches and Concepts of Power*, paper read April, 1977)

Thanks to Parham's jealousy and racial bias, this harmony was soon shattered. The founders of the Assemblies of God were fully committed to white Pentecostalism. One of the very purposes of tongues was completely ignored and another was substituted.

I believe one of the reasons the white founders wanted a separate organization is because they were uncomfortable with some of the physical responses by the African Americans to the outpouring of the Holy Spirit. It is my conviction that some of these responses were the result of inherited black culture and were not manifestations of the Spirit per se. Many of these black Americans were only one or two generations removed from their tribal ancestry in Africa and their tribal culture had been impressed

41

upon their minds from birth. These inculcations included responses one should make when in the presence of supernatural power. The Holy Spirit does not discard or ignore culture when he manifests His power. The Spirit delights in diverse cultures. Representatives from them all will populate heaven. John exults at the vision: *"There before me was a great multitude that no one could count, from every nation, tribe, people and language standing before the throne and in front of the Lamb."*(Revelation 7:9)

One of the many mistakes made by Western missionaries was that they tried to implant their own culture along with Christianity. (The very first Christians attempted to do that with their Jewish culture.) Modern missiologists have discovered the best way (perhaps the only way) to win the world for Jesus Christ is to permit people groups to retain all aspects of their culture that are not antithetical to the Lordship of Jesus. American Indians can retain their tribal dances, drums and pow wows in dedicated worship of Jesus Christ; Muslims can worship on Friday; Gypsies can dance before the Lord. None of these would be authentic worship expressions for me.

Dr. Donald McGavran, founder of the School of World Missions at Fuller Theological Seminary, has summed it up well: *"To Christianize a whole people, the first thing not to do is snatch individuals out of it (culture) into a different society. Peoples become Christians where a Christward movement occurs within that society. Bishop J.W. Pickett, in his important study Christ's Way to India's Heart' says: 'The process of extracting individuals from their setting in Hindu or Muslim communities does not build a church. On the contrary it arouses antagonism against Christianity and builds barriers against the spread of the gospel.'"*

I don't think our forebears understood this principle. I know I didn't until recent years.

Dr. McGavran then goes on to say: *Obviously the Christianization of a people requires reborn men and women...While the new convert must remain within his people, he must also experience the new birth...The power of any People Movement in Christ depends in great measure on the number of truly converted persons in it...There is no substitute for justification by faith or for the gift of the Holy Spirit."* (D.A. McGavran, The Bridges of God, Perspectives Reader, p. 336-7)

AN INVASION OF ANTI-SUPERNATURALISM

The liberal churches had been captured by rationalism long ago. In their view, supernaturalism was not possible; therefore, whatever was happening at Azusa Street was not miraculous. Period. I did not realize how deeply anti-supernaturalism had invaded liberal theology until the Navy selected me to study at Princeton Seminary in 1967. I loved my year of graduate study at Princeton and will say more about it later. There was a wide diversity of theological views represented among the professors, from conservative to extreme liberal.

One of the liberal professors was Dr. Paul Scherer, who had been pastor of Holy Trinity Lutheran Church in New York City for twenty-five years. In 1944, he accepted appointment as Brown Professor of Homiletics at Union Seminary in New York City, a stronghold of liberalism. While at Union he was selected to be Associate Editor of Exposition for the New Testament edition of The Interpreter's Bible published in 1951. After fifteen years at Union, he was appointed as the Patton Professor of Homiletics at Princeton Seminary. He was a superstar in the liberal firmament, so when I had the rare opportunity to enroll in one of his classes, I grabbed it.

Dr. Scherer was a gentle, urbane gentleman scholar who took a personal interest in his students. I developed a genuine respect for him as a person if not for his theological position. One of the assignments he gave me was to read and critique a newly-published book dealing with the resurrection of Jesus.

When I was at the Baptist Seminary in Denver, the theology of Karl Barth was about as liberal as we explored. The author of the book I was assigned made Barth look like an archconservative. I was appalled at the crassness with which the writer dismissed the reality of Jesus' bodily resurrection, completely failing to deal with any of the historical data that supported it. His argument essentially could be summarized like this:

- Miracles are impossible.
- For Jesus to return bodily alive after dying would necessitate a miracle.
- Therefore, it is impossible to have a bodily resurrection. As you can see, he advanced the classical arguments of anti-

supernaturalists such as Spinoza and Hume. It is an invalid circular argument still used by many who discount miracles.

I gave what I thought was a very scholarly critique from a conservative theological point of view. I pointed out the author's total failure to deal substantively with the New Testament text that affirmed a bodily resurrection. He failed to address the dynamic that led the early disciples to affirm a bodily resurrection despite persecution unto death. Instead of grappling with the historical data, the author presented some psychobabble about the disciples' mental state that led to their false assumption that Jesus had literally risen from the dead. It had no substance and I flatly stated so.

Dr. Scherer's response to my critique left me bewildered and saddened. He lamented that despite all modern scholarship, I still believed that Jesus arose bodily from the dead. I heard that Dr. Scherer was suffering at that time from cancer and died not too long afterwards. I pray that he is in heaven today. I am sure one glimpse of the nail scars in the resurrected body of his Savior radically altered his theology. It did for Thomas.

ARGUING AWAY THE SUPERNATURAL

Most of the liberal churches, such as Dr. Scherer represented, ignored reports of the miraculous from Los Angeles. The secular world ridiculed it as religious fanaticism gone amok. The imbedded tradition of the conservative evangelical cessationist churches was threatened and their leaders vigorously attacked the Pentecostal outpouring as being unbiblical or, worse, demonic. Participants declared that God had indeed restored the wondrous gifts of the Holy Spirit to the church. There were several possible choices.

• There was some kind of mass hysteria involved or some other natural explanation.

• It was supernatural but not from God. It was demonic.

• It was a divine manifestation. The spiritual gifts had indeed been restored to the church. Each possibility will be considered. Where does the evidence lead?

Hysteria as a neurological symptom came into prominence near the end of the nineteenth century as a result of Freud's psychological study. His preferred term was "conversion disorder," and it had nothing to do with religious conversion. It had its origin in Freud's contention that inner anxiety was converted into physical symptoms, hence, a conversion disorder. This apparently was the explanation by much of the secular world. It was also the explanation of choice for liberal Christianity since miracles were not an option, whether demonic or divine. I don't doubt there might have been incidents of hysteria, i.e., conversion disorder. But to suggest that thousands of people scattered across the world from many different backgrounds, races and ages were victims of conversion disorder is too preposterous for consideration. It would require a miracle. Unthinkable!

THE REVIVAL PHENOMENON CONTINUES

No doubt, many evangelical leaders hoped that the revival phenomenon in Los Angeles would prove to be a passing fad. If so, their hopes were soon dashed. The revival spread across the United States and throughout the world. Cessationists were faced with a difficult problem. The very spiritual gifts (charismata), which they taught had ceased when the apostles died, were being manifested throughout the world.

WHY ARE TRADITIONS SO HARD TO BREAK?

I believe the doctrine that the gifts had ceased had transmuted into a tradition. A tradition is more difficult to change than a doctrine if the doctrine comes out of an accepted authority that all can refer to. The accepted authority for evangelicals is the Bible. The cessationists' attempt to find a proof text led them to 1 Corinthians 13:8-10, to which I referred previously. Here is how their convoluted interpretation of this passage went: "The 'perfection' mentioned in verse ten ("But when perfection comes, the imperfect disappears") refers to the completion of the New Testament canon. When that happens, prophecy, languages (tongues) and knowledge will pass away because we have the inspired canon."

The Greek word *teleion*, translated "perfect" or "perfection," is used numerous times in the New Testament but never as a synonym for the New Testament canon. It usually speaks of the complete, full development of Christ-like character which is the ultimate goal of every Christian.

The context makes plain that this is what Paul has in mind here. Perfection comes when we stand in His presence transformed at last into His very image. "Now we see but a poor reflection as in a mirror; then we shall see face to face. Now I know in part; then I shall know fully, even as I am fully known." (1 Corinthians 13:12) That will be perfection, indeed!

Why did the cessationists not simply admit that a sovereign God had apparently restored supernatural spiritual gifts to His church? I suggest two reasons:

1) They had become more influenced by our materialistic, Western culture than they realized. The supernatural embarrassed them. They wanted to retain control of their theological kingdom, and the Holy Spirit's activity threatened them.

2) Another reason, and perhaps more prevalent, is that cessationists bought into a centuries-old tradition and traditions are extremely difficult to disengage from. Egos become immersed in them.

One can alter doctrinal positions, if the Scripture convinces him he should. I certainly have changed some of mine as I have matured in understanding Scripture. But religious traditions become part of our spiritual DNA. If one departs from them, he feels like he is losing his identity. Scripture will not produce a change of direction because the belief is not founded on Scripture but on a traditional interpretation of Scripture. Tradition wins out over exegesis. It was tradition that closed the minds of the Pharisees and prompted them to plot the death of Jesus. Any threat to tradition must be destroyed. It was tradition that drove Saul of Tarsus to terrorism and murder—nothing less than the Damascus Road experience could have shaken him free.

In their efforts to hold onto a sacred tradition, cessationists dismissed examples of charismatic gifts as being misrepresented, exaggerated or false reports. Others actually declared that if there were indeed such examples, they were demonic in origin.

After I had gained the confidence of my fellow students at the Conservative Baptist Seminary in Denver, some shared with me that they had been taught that speaking in tongues was demonic. The fact that they were sharing this with me convinced me they had not bought into this teaching. As the "token Pentecostal," they just wanted to pick my brain. I never argued but just let my life and scholarship speak for me. I treasure the friendships that came out of those days.

I must say that our cessationist critics are not wholly wrong. They have had reason to be critical of some representations of the Pentecostal movement. Pentecostals' mistaken view of the purpose of tongues has contributed to abuses and disunity. Reports of miracles have at times been misrepresented, some blatantly exaggerated and some simply not true. I deal at greater length with such abuses in chapter ten.

GENUINE SPIRITUAL ACTIVITY CANNOT BE SUPRESSED

Admittedly, the Azusa Street revival reached people very much like the Corinthian believers described by Paul:

"Brothers, think of what you were when you were called. Not many of you were wise by human standards; not many were influential; not many were of noble birth. But God chose the foolish things of the world to shame the wise; God chose the weak things of the world to shame the strong. He chose the lowly things of the world and the despised things—and the things that are not— to nullify the things that are, so that no one may boast before him." (1 Corinthians 1:26-29)

Think of it. The black preacher who led the Azusa Street revival was the son of slaves and the church was a converted horse stable. The congregation was predominantly black with a hodgepodge of poor whites, Asians, and Hispanics, with a smattering of educated and wealthy. The opponents had a heyday ridiculing and belittling the emerging Pentecostal movement. Certainly, some abuses were evident, just as in the Corinthian church. But God was at the heart of this revival of spiritual gifts.

The gifts were genuine and most participants were genuinely hungry for the Holy Spirit's presence and power. God responded and the church world was startled by another Pentecost. It could not be contained by those who opposed it. It started with hundreds, in a short time it was thousands, then tens of thousands, then millions.

When I enrolled in seminary in 1954, the movement numbered

tens of millions. By this time the Pentecostal constituency within the United States had largely graduated to middle-class status, much of it due to an improved economy. Although the clergy were becoming more educated, mainly through Bible schools, there were still many pastors who entered the ministry without formal theological education.

My dad, born in 1902, entered the Assemblies of God ministry with only an eighth-grade education, but he immersed himself in Scripture and was a keen Bible scholar. There were many others like him from his generation. They may have lacked formal education but what they did have was a powerful, life-transforming encounter with Jesus Christ. It was Jesus who had baptized them in His Spirit and sent them forth to bear witness to the Baptizer and the baptism. They did this boldly in the face of much opposition and, sometimes, persecution.

The huge and rapid numerical increase of Pentecostal believers made it more difficult for cessationists to continue insisting the spiritual gifts had ceased. In the United States, but more particularly from mission fields, came verified reports of "signs and wonders" manifested wherever the Pentecostal message was proclaimed. The reports were too numerous and well validated to deny. Some cessationists fell back on the theory known as "concentric cessation." This theory proposes that the gifts of the Spirit were withdrawn from areas where the church was established. However, they may temporarily be restored for missionary activity to validate the gospel in unreached areas.

This is another theory with no scriptural basis. But at least it is a concession because it acknowledges the reality of spiritual gifts.

THE CHARISMATIC RENEWAL WITHIN MAINLINE CHURCHES

On April 3, 1960, a bombshell exploded within the church world. Dennis Bennett, pastor of 2600-member St. Mark's Episcopal Church in Van Nuys, California, announced from the pulpit that he had been baptized in the Holy Spirit. As he shared his experience with the parishioners, there was a mixed response. Some were genuinely curious and wanted to explore this spiritual dimension. Others reacted negatively and some of his vestrymen suggested he resign.

The media saw this as a major religious news event and reported it as such. Both *Newsweek* and *Time* magazines featured articles about it. Rather than subject the church to such zealous media scrutiny, Pastor Bennett decided he should resign. Shortly afterwards, he was invited to become pastor of St. Luke's Episcopal Church in Ballard, Washington, near Seattle. It was a small, nearly defunct parish when Dennis Bennett became vicar.

Amazingly, his bishop fully supported his message and his experience, as did his small congregation. Invited by his bishop to speak to all the Anglican priests in his jurisdiction, he did so and twelve of them were baptized in the Holy Spirit.

Visitors began to pour into St. Luke's to see and hear what was happening. Before long it was necessary to have three services on Sunday morning and another in the evening to accommodate the crowds; the sanctuary was so small it scarcely seated two hundred. Pastor Bennett greeted, preached to, and taught the visitors, but he always urged them to return to their own churches. And the visitors kept coming and coming and coming. Many mainline churches were represented in addition to Epicopal— Presbyterian, Lutheran, Reformed and others. My neighbors immediately behind me have told me of their participation in St. Luke's.

To distinguish this move from the Pentecostal outpouring on Azusa Street, it was commonly called the Charismatic Renewal. The gifts of the Spirit were manifested similarly in both. There was, however, a significant difference. Those who experienced the Azusa Street Pentecostal experience were driven from their churches and, as a consequence, were forced to organize separate fellowships or denominations. On the other hand, Dennis Bennett and other charismatic leaders urged mainline members who were baptized in the Holy Spirit to remain in their own churches and bear witness to what God was doing in their lives. And there was one other difference. Speaking in tongues was practiced by many but it was not necessarily the initial physical evidence of being filled with the Spirit.

The cessationists now had a new problem to overcome to sustain their contention that spiritual gifts were withdrawn from the church at the end of the apostolic age. It was no longer unsophisticated peasants who were being baptized in the Holy Spirit and receiving spiritual gifts. Now highly-educated, theologically trained elites from mainline churches were receiving the same experience.

Because of more mature spiritual oversight usually received by those involved in the Charismatic Renewal, there were fewer abuses or counterfeits to criticize. However, cessationists were not deterred from advancing the same arguments as before. Since cessationism had morphed into a sacred tradition, it apparently would take more than Scripture and validating miracles to change minds and hearts. But God would keep trying. Another powerful move of the Holy Spirit was about to erupt.

THE SPIRIT DEFIES DENOMINATIONAL LINES

In February, 1967, there was dramatic invasion by the Holy Spirit into the Roman Catholic Church. During a retreat, professors and students at Duquesne University had been studying two books, the Acts of the Apostles in the New Testament and *The Cross and the Switchblade* by David Wilkerson. These books, and no doubt reports about the Holy Spirit's activity among "the separated brethren," had created a thirst for an outpouring of the Holy Spirit such as was described in Acts and demonstrated in the ministry of David Wilkerson among gangs in New York City. God satisfied that thirst by baptizing Duquesne professors and students in the Holy Spirit. The operation of the gifts of the Spirit was witnessed with joy and wonder. The renewal quickly spread to Notre Dame and from there to Catholic campuses across the country.

There is exciting new data that makes the Church increasingly aware that cessationism is out of touch with reality. John MacArthur, leading proponent of this doctrine, still contends that the supernatural gifts of the Holy Spirit were withdrawn from the Church at the end of the apostolic age. He has no biblical foundation for this position and tries to manufacture one from 1 Corinthians 13: 8-10. He insists that the "perfection" which makes the gifts of prophecy, tongues and knowledge obsolete is the formulation of the New Testament. But if knowledge has passed away, where did he get his knowledge concerning tongues? The simple truth is, as multitudes of Bible scholars recognize, Paul equates the "perfect" with when we shall see our Lord "face to face" and are no longer compelled to see only a dim reflection of His glory.

Since he has no Scripture to reinforce his position, MacArthur attacks his opponents with many examples of abuse and misuse of spiritual gifts, particularly of tongues. I certainly agree that abuse and misuse have occurred and still occur. I relate elsewhere some that I have witnessed personally. But these are mostly aberrations and not typical. However, he never actually deals with the real issue of whether the supernatural gifts of the Spirit are operating in the Church today, either from a bona fide biblical or historical basis. I have pointed out MacArthur's lack of biblical support for his position. Now I want to present data from the empirical, historical viewpoint.

Today there is a far greater manifestation of God's supernatural power in many areas of the world than when I was in Princeton Seminary. Dr. Craig S. Keener has recently written a monumental account of what is happening, particularly in Africa, Asia, and Latin America. Traveling around the world and interviewing many diverse Christians, he has compiled case histories of all kinds of miracles but especially physical healings. Following is just a small sample from this eleven-hundred-page, two-volume work entitled simply *Miracles.*

Here is an account of miracles among Anglicans in Singapore:

"These healings have occurred . . . in the Anglican Church in Singapore. Some traditional Anglicans were suspicious when the charismatic movement came to Singapore in the early 1970's, partly due to unhealthy experiences in the past. Nevertheless, that movement caught on, with attendant spiritual gifts including healings. In 1972, Bishop Chiu Ban It, Singapore's first indigenous Bishop, experienced a dramatic encounter with God through this movement and unexpectedly found himself gifted in praying for healing. The Reverend Dr. Michael Green, now advisor in evangelism to the archbishops of Canterbury and York, and senior research fellow at Wycliffe Hall, Oxford, notes what he witnessed firsthand there in 1973. As the bishop prayed, Green saw 'physical healings of an incontrovertible nature—I think of a man throwing away his crutches, and another whose hearing was restored. The

healing services became the catalyst for a new commitment to evangelism, with signs and wonders accompanying the evangelism, and healings also continued as part of church life. Such factors eventually contributed to the young Anglican Province of South East Asia being 'one of the fastest growing parts of the Anglican Communion.'

"An Anglican convert from a non-Christian background, Soh Chye Ann, faced significant opposition from his family. His sister, however, was dying, and neither hospitals nor temples proved able to help her. The family finally asked if the Christians could help; they prayed fervently, 'and a miraculous, complete and instantaneous healing took place' in front of the family, whom immediately became Christians. Singapore's Anglican Church sent Chye Ann and his wife as missionaries to South Africa, where they worked successfully for ethnic and social reconciliation in Durban. He is now the Asia director for the Anglican Church Mission Society in London." (Craig S. Keener, *Miracles*, pp. 273-74)

Let me quote summary statements from some Christian leaders in other areas of Asia.

MALAYSIA: *"Western theology invariably asks the question: Are miracles possible? This, of course, addresses the Enlightenment problem of a closed universe. In much of Asia, that is a non-question because the miraculous is assumed and fairly regularly experienced."* (Hwa Yung, bishop of Malaysian Methodist Church and former Principal of Maylasia Theological Seminary, quoted by Keener, 264)

CHINA: *"All Christian churches in China practice some form of healing, including Three-Self churches. In fact, according to some surveys, 90% of new believers cite healing as a reason for their conversion."* (Edmond Tang in his book *Healers*, p. 481, Keener p. 264)

INDIA: *"In Gujarat and Maharashtra, many tangible miracles have happened, such as the healing of the deaf and dumb and incurable diseases, which strengthened the ministry in its initial stage."* (Abraham Pothen, author of *Missions* 189, Keener p. 264)

I think it is obvious as to what has produced sincere, but mistaken, Evangelical cessationists in the Western world:

First, they have seen no supernatural gifts operating in their own ministry or in that of many of their contemporaries. Therefore, they conclude that the gifts are no longer operative in the Church. I grant you that this doctrine was formed before the present day explosion of miracles has made cessationism obviously false. It illustrates the danger of building doctrine with the absence of scriptural support.

Second, although the supernatural gifts of the Spirit accompanied the outpouring of the Holy Spirit at Azusa street in 1906, most Evangelical churches rejected them for two reasons:

1. The predominant Pentecostal position concerning tongues as the required evidence of Spirit baptism was clearly without a biblical foundation. Good, sincere Berean exegetes of Scripture could see this and rejected the doctrine. What they didn't see was that the gift of tongues was scriptural and legitimate. It was the purpose Pentecostals assigned to tongues that was invalid. They threw the baby out with the bath water and missed a rich blessing.

2. Abuse and misuse of tongues and other gifts was associated with Pentecostals. They feared being tarred with the brush that labeled them "Pentecostal." If we Pentecostals had acknowledged the unifying purpose of tongues as symbols of all peoples from the beginning, I am convinced the United States would have seen an interdenominational acceptance of miracles as the norm.

This explosion of miracles is transdenominational. Unfortunately, it is muted in the United States and western Europe. But even here there is an increasing hunger for God's power to be manifested. Cessationists are having to acknowledge that the supernatural gifts of the Holy Spirit have not been withdrawn from the Church. Keener makes a brief note of this before describing significant healings at Taylor University: *"Bill Heth, a professor at Taylor University and formerly a cessationist, noted that various healings have occurred on their campus."* (Ibid. p. 441) Reality trumps unbiblical religious theory or tradition.

When the Charismatic Renewal invaded the Catholic Church, I was senior chaplain at the Marine Corps Air Station at Beaufort, South Carolina. After less than a year at this assignment, I received notification that I had been selected for a year of postgraduate study at a major graduate school of my choice. I had been selected for a Regular Navy commission five years previously; this was another indication that the Navy Chaplains Corps had marked me as a candidate for future advancement and responsibility. I was grateful and excited. It was a wonderful opportunity and I wanted to make the most of it. It was my obligation to choose my field of study and I considered the fields of marriage or family counseling. I met with a committee at Duke University to talk about this, but they discouraged me from pursuing this field.

The senior chaplain in Washington who oversaw the post-graduate program asked me to come see him. He was a lovable but crusty Southern Baptist nearing the end of his chaplaincy career. He invited me into his office and shared his heart.

"Glenn, the Navy has a surplus of counselors and we don't need another one. I recommend that you not pursue that course of study. What the chaplaincy needs is good proclaimers of the gospel. I suggest that you investigate theological schools that can hone and refine your preaching skills."

I took his suggestion as divine direction and began acting on it. I found no major seminary with a better reputation for hermeneutics (the art and science of interpreting Scripture) than Princeton Theological Seminary. I requested and received official orders to report to Princeton Seminary for a course of study in hermeneutics and liturgics beginning in September, 1967.

PENTECOSTAL/CHARISMATIC WITNESS AT PRINCETON SEMINARY

Princeton was the fountainhead of evangelical cessationism. Dr. Benjamin B. Warfield, renowned Princeton theologian of late nineteenth and early twentieth century, wrote an influential book, *Counterfeit Miracles*, in support of cessationism. The venerable Doctor would have turned over in his grave if he could have seen what was happening on his beloved seminary campus fifty years later.

I reported to Princeton in August to locate housing and get Celia, our eight-year-old daughter, enrolled in third grade. Four other Navy chaplains had also been selected for a course of study at Princeton. Frankly, I was quite surprised at the amount of Charismatic Renewal activity on campus. Presbyterianism had been significantly impacted by this outpouring of the Spirit upon

54

mainline churches. There were groups of Spirit-filled students meeting evenings in homes for prayer and fellowship. On campus there were charismatic students who met for prayer during lunch hour. If the weather was favorable, they met outside on the lawn and you could see them scattered about the grounds praying or engaging in discussion. When inclement or cold weather forced them inside, they occasionally ran into opposition from professors who did not want them invading their turf. But there was never any official opposition from the administration.

I was told that these charismatic prayer groups were largely the result of the ministry of Peter John Marshall, the son of Peter and Catherine Marshall, while he was a student at Princeton. He had graduated a year or two prior to my arrival. His father had been the beloved chaplain of the U.S. Senate who died at age forty-six of a heart attack when Peter John was nine years old. Catherine Marshall, a skilled and prolific writer, wrote a moving biographical story about her late husband entitled *A Man Called Peter*. A best seller, it later was made into a popular movie.

Catherine had a very personal and moving encounter with Jesus Christ that culminated with her being baptized in the Holy Spirit. She used her writing skills to gently lead people into a scriptural experience of this baptismal ministry of Jesus referred to by John the Baptist in Mark 1:7-8 and by Jesus in Acts 1:5. Peter John Marshall had experienced this baptism in the Holy Spirit and shared the good news with fellow students at Princeton. Although I never took a leading part in these charismatic campus and home groups, I did visit and participate in them from time to time. It became known that one of the Navy chaplains attending the Seminary was Pentecostal.

The year at Princeton was intellectually stimulating and required plenty of discipline and hard work, as I soon discovered. Dr. Bruce Metzger, one of the world's leading Greek scholars, was offering a course on Paul's letter to the Galatians. I couldn't pass up the chance to study under this renowned scholar so I signed up for the course. On the first day in class, Dr. Metzger announced in his inimitable, gentle way, "Now, ladies and gentlemen, I must tell you this is not a class for beginners in New Testament Greek. I am going to give a test to measure your proficiency in the language. If it is not adequate, you must choose another course."

I had taken four years of Greek in Denver Seminary but ten years had passed. I had not made the study of Greek a priority in the intervening years so I took the test with considerable trepidation. When I was filing out of class the next day, Dr. Metzger called me aside and said softly, "Mr. Brown, I suggest that you enroll in another class. It is early in the quarter and you should have no problem." It was obvious that I had failed the entrance exam but I was not about to admit defeat so quickly. I pleaded my case.

"Dr. Metzger, I have been out of seminary ten years and my knowledge of Greek has slipped a little. Just give me a chance to take one more test and if I fail, I'll enroll in another class."

He hesitated and then with obvious reluctance he agreed. The good doctor had gotten my attention and I immersed myself in the Greek text of Galatians prior to the next test. I parsed verbs, checked vocabulary in the lexicon, memorized rules of grammar, and got a friend to grill me. I took the test again, feeling much more confident than the first time. Eureka! When my second test was returned, it sported a red "A" at the top. Hard work and persistence had paid off. They usually do.

Dr. McCleod headed the homiletics department and helped guide my course of study. He was a fine clinician, able to critique sermons and give helpful suggestions for improvement. Members of his class had to prepare sermons to present before a committee composed of professors from the various disciplines in the Seminary. Afterwards, we had to endure critiques from these august scholars from the viewpoint he or she represented, whether it was theology, counseling, Christian education, or others. Sometimes it was painful but always beneficial.

I was surprised and greatly honored during my last quarter at Princeton to be invited to occupy the pulpit of historic Miller Chapel for one of the chapel services. I never did know who was responsible for this invitation. Perhaps it was Dr. McCleod. I struggled for a while concerning a subject but not very long. A Pentecostal chaplain had been invited to preach so somebody must have wanted a Pentecostal sermon. I preached on the ministry of the Holy Spirit as recorded in both Old and New Testaments. Try to do that in twenty minutes! Dr. James McCord, President of the Seminary, was the liturgist. After the service while we were taking off our clerical robes, he said to me, "Chaplain, Princeton needs more preaching like that."

Dr. Hope, Professor in the Old Testament Department, also approached me. We had never met, though I had seen him on campus and knew who he was. It soon became apparent he didn't know who I was. All the chaplains wore civilian clothes so there was nothing to identify us with the military. He presumed I was a Presbyterian pastor and struck up a conversation. "Where is your church located, Pastor?" I explained who I was and what brought me to Princeton. I'm still not quite sure whether it was a compliment for a Pentecostal preacher to be mistaken for a Presbyterian pastor. But why not? There were plenty of Presbyterians involved in the Charismatic Renewal.

In June, 1968, I completed my postgraduate studies and could now tack a Master of Theology (Th.M.) to my pedigree. In the midst of all the doctorates being conferred, it wasn't particularly impressive, but at least my mother thought it was great. I was just extremely grateful for the opportunity. I was pleased that I had finished with an excellent academic record, hadn't embarrassed the Navy, and had a better foundation for future ministry. I had already received orders to my next assignment aboard a helicopter carrier bound for Vietnam. Little did I realize that my experience in Vietnam would precipitate an internal theological struggle that would threaten my ministry as a Navy Chaplain.

All that I have written thus far is but prelude to this struggle. Here is a short postscript to my Princeton experience. Ten years later, shortly after my retirement from the Navy, I received letters from two of my former classmates, the first from an influential Presbyterian pastor in Alabama. We had become good friends while we were students together and had remained in contact over the years. He wanted me to know about a Presbyterian church in his region that needed a pastor. He asked me to consider being a candidate and gave me the name and address of the gentleman who chaired the search committee. I did write him, but respectfully declined to be considered as I knew some doctrinal issues might create problems. Furthermore, I had already accepted the challenge of being installed as pastor of the small, struggling Assemblies of God church in Pleasanton, California.

The second letter came out of the blue from another fellow classmate of whom I had no recollection. Here is the gist of his letter:

Dear Chaplain,

When we were in Princeton together, I opposed everything you stood for. But I want you to know that I have been baptized in the Holy Spirit. I meet weekly with a group of charismatic Presbyterian pastors for prayer and mutual encouragement. Thank you for your faithful witness even when opposed by people like me.

I treasure both letters.

I enjoyed the academic climate at Princeton. I depended heavily upon the Holy Spirit to help me discern truth from error. The only class the Navy requested that I take was one that portrayed the religious culture of Vietnam. Otherwise, I was given freedom to select my classes and professors. I can truthfully say I was enriched by each.

I deliberately chose one class taught by a well-known, ultra-liberal professor. It was an enlightening experience and revealed the power of tradition divorced from an honest search for truth. In this case the tradition was the theory advanced by anti-supernaturalists (Spinoza, Hume, materialistic evolutionists and the like) who deny the possibility of miracles. I have described elsewhere my experience with this professor. But even this class was profitable. It gave me firsthand experience of the shallowness and closed-mindedness of those who dismiss miracles a priori. It also revealed to me the binding power of religious tradition that is opposed by the truth of Scripture.

I was about to discover the tenacity of what I was convinced was unscriptural religious tradition at the other end of the theological spectrum. To my consternation and distress, it was in my own church. The theological battle that ensued coincided with the military battle that was raging in Vietnam. In the pages that follow I will describe some of my experiences in each arena.

CHAPTER 5

A CONSCIENCE PROBED IN VIETNAM

THE YEAR WAS 1969. The place was the USS Okinawa (LPH-3), a helicopter carrier engaged in counter-offensive combat operations against the Vietcong and North Vietnamese troops near Da Nang off the coast of South Vietnam. This bathtub-shaped launching pad for helicopters was loaded with heavily armed Marines. The carrier had been my home since I had come aboard as ship's chaplain in July, 1968. On November 2, 1968, we sailed for Vietnam, cruising at twenty knots. In late November we anchored in the Da Nang harbor, preparing to take aboard approximately two thousand heavily armed "guests."

OKI-3, as she was affectionately called, was the flagship for Amphibious Squadron Five. Our senior "guest" was the Commodore with his staff of twenty officers; another sixteen hundred guests were Marines who comprised Special Landing Force Alpha under the command of a battle-experienced colonel. Battalion Landing Team 2/26 was the major combat force of SLF Alpha. These were the troops ferried in-country by "choppers" to engage enemy forces. Marine Medium Helicopter Squadron 362 was tasked with flying the Marines into battle. They employed twenty-five helicopters with air and ground crews to accomplish their mission. In addition, there were two medical units assigned. One was a skilled surgical team with five surgeons and thirteen assistants who could handle anything short of brain surgery. Another team of three general practitioners plus twenty-two corpsmen cared for less serious wounds and illnesses. There was a 100-bed hospital ward to house wounded returned from combat.

The same choppers that carried Marines into combat returned the wounded to the ship. During combat operations everyone in ship's company had an assigned battle station. The chaplain's station was on the flight deck where it was easier to greet the incoming wounded, most of whom were victims of booby traps and personnel mines.

Confronted by the horror and destructiveness of war, I became very aware of my own mortality. I was actually in a safe

59

environment while aboard ship—the bad guys were on shore. I sometimes felt guilty about not sharing the danger of the young men in combat and sought opportunities to go ashore whenever possible. One such opportunity involved a twelve-year-old Vietnamese girl who lost her leg just below the knee after being trapped in cross fire between American and Vietcong forces.

Our surgical team wanted to sponsor her for a prosthesis and asked me to go to her village and seek her parents' permission to transport her to a facility for the procedure. The Marine assigned to fly me into the village was a veteran combat helicopter pilot. I put on the protective armor usually worn when going in-country and carried my only weapon—an 8 mm movie camera. After lifting off the OKI-3 deck, the pilot flew high enough over the green jungle to stay out of range of small arms fire. When we were over the landing zone, he spiraled down swiftly so that we would not be an easy target for enemy snipers.

The girl's parents listened intently as my interpreter and I carefully explained what we wished to do. After a brief conference, they smiled and said they would gladly accept our offer. While they made the necessary preparations for their daughter to leave, the villagers gave me a tour of the village. They were especially eager to show off their school. The facilities were crude and primitive but the children were precious, like children everywhere.

A MILITARY STYLE WAKE-UP CALL

We were on the ground no more than half an hour. The chopper crew remained with their bird as the pilot let the engine idle. With the aid of a single crutch and village friends, the crippled girl made her way to the entry hatch of the chopper. I saw the makings of a great human interest story so I paused to record the scene with my movie camera. This incensed the Marine pilot who chewed me out in very salty language, emphasizing that every second on the ground was a dangerous second, especially after being in one place so long. The angry Major growled that even a short delay could jeopardize lives. It was a sobering lesson for me and I took it to heart.

This and other in-country experiences made me increasingly aware that war can suddenly produce death and destruction to the unwary. It forced me to search my conscience and ask myself, "Glenn, are you ready to die?" It wasn't a question of salvation. No, it was a matter of resolving an issue with my church that I found painful to face because serious consequences could result. However, I didn't want to suddenly appear before God with unfinished business between us, so I knew I had to "bite the bullet."

God had been probing my conscience about being honest with the Assemblies of God, my ecclesiastical endorsing agency. Let me explain. Every minister granted credentials by the Assemblies of God must submit an annual credential renewal form that required one to acknowledge agreement with all the denomination's statements of "fundamental truths." My study of Scripture had led me question one of the statements. This is the statement that troubled me:

"The baptism of believers in the Holy Spirit is witnessed by the initial physical sign of speaking with other tongues as the Spirit of God gives them utterance."

I determined to be as forthright as possible when I dealt with this issue on my next credential renewal form. Ironically, I knew that to do so might cost me my career as a Navy chaplain. If I were dropped from the Assemblies of God, dismissal from the Navy Chaplains' Corps would surely follow. This could create dire consequences for my wife and daughter. Loss of income could be recouped elsewhere but retirement and medical coverage would be difficult to replace. Believe me, I did not take this lightly. I believed God had called me into the chaplaincy and I loved this ministry. But I was also convinced that God was directing me to be open and honest with the Assemblies of God about a phase of doctrine I could no longer fully subscribe to in good conscience. The consequences must be left in His hands.

By no means was the Marine chopper pilot the only person who sensitized me to my mortality and my need to have everything "squared away" with God. Other men and events affected me much deeper emotionally. In the midst of war and death, I was learning important lessons about life, lessons about integrity and about making tough, costly decisions. These cumulatively hardened my determination to resolve the doctrinal issue with my denomination and let the chips fall where they may.

A NAVY CORPSMAN TEACHES ME ABOUT INTEGRITY

There are some people you know all too well and would like to forget; there are others you meet in passing but will remember forever. "Doc" is one of the latter. It's been forty-plus years since I last saw him and time has erased his given name, if I ever knew it. The Marines he so selflessly served called him "Doc" and that's how I'll always remember him.

Doc was a young Navy corpsman, possibly twenty-one years old, attached to BLT 2/26, the Marine infantry unit that was part of SLF Alpha. He wasn't a big man physically, maybe 5 feet 9 inches, 150 pounds, but he exuded gentle inner strength and moral toughness. A few freckles were scattered across a face that was topped by close-cropped sandy hair. He spoke with the soft, slow drawl of the Deep South. As I got to know him better, I discovered his Christian faith ran deep without any tinge of self-righteousness. I first met Doc on the crowded hanger deck of USS Okinawa as the units of BLT 2/26 prepared to board the helicopters for a vertical assault on the Vietcong's turf. Somehow, amidst the organized confusion and din of milling troops and clamoring machines, he found me as I watched the embarking routine.

Approaching me, he eagerly asked, "Sir, can we have a few moments together alone?" "Sure," I responded. "Let's find a place with a little more privacy." I led him to an area of the ship where the noise was less intense and waited for him to speak.

"Chaplain, we're going into combat in a few minutes and some of my Marines are going to get hit. Sir, they are going to call for me to help them and I've got to get to them, sir. Will you pray that God will help me reach them in time and give them the aid they need?

"I'm going to need His help, sir."

A chaplain receives many prayer requests—requests for safety and protection, for family members, for sweethearts—but Doc was unique in his selflessness. At a time of great personal danger in an environment of kill-or-be-killed, he earnestly prayed that he might be a messenger of life. That was it. His only request was that he might not fail a wounded man who needed his life-saving skill.

I led in a simple, short prayer: "Our Father, giver of life, Doc wants to serve you by saving and preserving lives. Use him as your angel of mercy amidst the dangers of battle. In Christ's name, amen." With an easy smile Doc thanked me, shook my hand and left to board the chopper.

In a few days the combat operation was completed and the wounded were safely aboard in the hospital ward. The others were in the ship's troop compartments enjoying a brief respite from the stress and danger of battle. BLT 2/26 had its own chaplain who conducted services when the troops were in the field, but when the troops were aboard the OKI-3, he relished being able to relax awhile and let me conduct the Protestant worship services for the troops. I enjoyed that because when the Marines were embarked, not only was attendance greatly increased but there was a greater sense of our dependence on God's grace and mercy. Doc was always at chapel services. He loved to worship and sing the great hymns of the church.

The very nature of the war against the Vietcong insurgents necessitated repeated sweeps through the same terrain. Our forces would drive them out and depart, but soon the enemy would infiltrate the area again and we would drive them out once more. This was the deadly cycle in which we were engaged.

After several days' rest from an operation, the Marines prepared for the next. Each time before he boarded his assigned chopper, Doc found me and requested our moment of prayer together. And always his request was the same. "Chaplain, sir, pray that God will enable me to reach my men when they call for my help." It was a hallowed moment. I was moved by Doc's selfless devotion to God and to the men he cared about so deeply.

Our six months on-station off Vietnam was broken into three segments of approximately two months each. After seven weeks on-station, the ship was ordered into Subic Bay for maintenance and a few days' rest for the crew. We were near the end of our second period on-station when Doc came to me after chapel service, displaying more excitement than usual.

"Chaplain, sir, I just noticed an electric organ secured above the hanger deck. I'm an organist and when we return from our next operation I'll play for chapel services." I had no idea Doc was a musician but I was thrilled at the prospect of having live organ music. "Doc," I beamed, "that is great. I can hardly wait for you to get back."

Just before the OKI-3 left for Subic Bay in March, 1969, the Marines went ashore for a major engagement and I had my usual special moment with Doc. "Don't forget," he reminded me, "when we come back aboard, I'm going to play the organ for chapel services."

"Doc," I replied, "not only will I not forget but I will never let you forget either." We shook hands and said our good-byes in anticipation of being together again soon.

When the OKI-3 returned from Subic Bay, it was a somber, battle-weary force of Marines that reboarded her. A heavy shroud of gloom permeated the atmosphere—and with good reason. Casualties had been heavy in the operation. I looked for Doc among the hundreds of troops milling about but was unable to spot him. A sense of foreboding enveloped me. I was sure something was seriously wrong.

As I made inquiries among the Marines, their fragmented accounts helped me piece together the story of Doc's final hours. His unit had come under heavy artillery fire and some men, wounded by shrapnel, had called for his help. As always, Doc ran to their aid. While he was tending their wounds, another artillery round came in and scored a direct hit, killing Doc and the men he was tending.

I was stunned by the news and filled with a sense of profound loss. Even today, forty years later, when I think of Doc it is with deep regret and sorrow that this talented young man was taken from us. But beyond that, his example of manly Christian love, his integrity, his service and sacrifice in the midst of a hellish war will always haunt and inspire me.

Somewhere in our country where people speak with a lilting Southern drawl, a family member or friend of Doc's may read this and say, "That sounds like my relative or my friend of years gone by." No doubt time has healed the raw hurt that first accompanied the news of your indescribable loss, but the scars will always be there. If by some miracle you happen to see this, I pray you will find comfort in knowing that someone else humbly and gratefully still remembers this unique godly man. Thank you for your investment of love, discipline, and gospel truth with which you so powerfully endowed Doc. He touched many lives with that rich heritage after he left your circle of protection.

Thank you and God bless you, whoever and wherever you are.

GREATER LOVE HAS NO MAN THAN THIS

I never knew the name of another young man who had a profound effect on me. One evening I was contacted by the Executive Officer who told me the following story:

"Chaplain, the body of a Marine killed in action has been flown in and placed in the morgue. It seems that the enemy lobbed a grenade into a hole where he and several of his buddies were taking cover. This Marine threw himself on the grenade and the force of the explosion blew his guts out and stripped off his clothing. We couldn't find his dog tags so we don't know any particulars about his religion. He may be Catholic, Protestant or even Jewish and, as you know, some religions require prayers to be said for the dead. Would you please go to the morgue and do whatever you chaplains do? By the way, all his fellow Marines survived."

Chaplains are taught what to do if they are required to substitute for a chaplain of a different faith. For example, if a Roman Catholic was presumed to be dying and there was no priest available, the Protestant chaplain could say, "I'm Chaplain Doe. There is no Catholic priest in the area but if he were here he would pray this prayer with you." The appropriate prayer would then be prayed. I was called upon to do this only once. But when the pertinent faith is unknown, what prayer is offered?

I went immediately to the morgue, a refrigerated space in a lower aft deck much like a large, walk-in freezer. Entering the compartment and closing the hatch behind me, I stood for a few moments taking in the scene. The stark white walls were illuminated by a bright ceiling light that shone on the eviscerated corpse stretched out before me.

This was my first visit to this haven for dead bodies and my mind was flooded with thoughts. What went on in the mind of this man in that split second before he launched his body on the grenade? Had he spiritually and emotionally prepared himself beforehand for this heroic act of self-sacrifice? Had he and his squad members ever discussed what they might do if confronted with a live enemy grenade? Or was this a completely spontaneous act birthed by an inexplicable love for the men with whom he served? I would never know.

I just knew this man had deliberately sacrificed his life so that his friends could live. I was humbled and awed by what he had done. The thought crossed my mind, "Could I have done what this Marine did?" I didn't know and prayed that I would never be put to such a test.

I had come to pray—but what kind of prayer? I truly felt as if I **was** standing on holy ground, but how should I address the Holy One? Prayers for the dead were not part of my repertoire. Scripture taught me that once the soul exits the body, the person is totally in the hands of God, beyond human influence. I could leave this young man with God in complete confidence.

But what about his family? Surely there were parents, perhaps grandparents, maybe brothers and sisters who would be devastated by the report of his death. I knew this was where I must focus my prayer. I cried out to God on behalf of the family members who would soon be grief-stricken when they received the death report. Concluding my prayer, I sensed the warmth of God's Spirit inside that cold morgue.

I took one final, reverent look at the body that spoke eloquently of the words of Jesus: "No one has greater love than the one who lays down his life for his friends." (John 15:13)

THE TRAGEDY OF THE USS FRANK E. EVANS

One other life-and-death situation had a deep impact on me personally, but in a less immediate way. Sometime in the spring of 1969, Captain Williams, skipper of the OKI-3, was contacted by the skipper of the USS Frank E. Evans, an American destroyer providing naval gunfire in support of our ground forces. The Evans asked if a chaplain could be provided by the OKI-3 to visit and conduct services aboard the destroyer. Our Captain informed me of the request and I was eager to go.

Since members of the crew on a destroyer are too few to rate a chaplain, religious lay leaders serve as efficiently as they can, but the service of a chaplain is welcome whenever possible. In this case, I'm not sure what prompted the request for a chaplain's visit but it may have been because the USS Evans was about to be relieved of her fire support duties and had orders to be part of a training exercise in the South China Sea, along with ships from Australia and New Zealand. A helicopter carrier was the logical ship from which to request a chaplain, since a helicopter must be employed to deliver the chaplain.

I embarked on our ship's helicopter, generally referred to as a "Holy Helo" when the chaplain was on board for a mission. We flew directly to the USS Evans and hovered overhead briefly while the deck crew prepared to receive me on board. I was already in a harness attached to a winch cable waiting for the right moment to exit the chopper hatch. This was my first time to be lowered to a ship by cable.

Wave action caused the destroyer to pitch and roll slightly; heavy rolls could be hazardous. If the ship rose as the cable was descending there was a chance of serious injury. At a signal from the winch operator, I slipped out the hatch and began my descent.

The operator timed my arrival so I met the deck at just the right time. It was a piece of cake! Quickly removing the harness and giving the helicopter crew a "thumbs up," I turned to greet the sailors waiting to welcome me. The chopper would return the next day to retrieve me. I wandered around the ship, visiting the various work spaces of the officers and crew. I wanted to see as many men as possible so they would know a chaplain was on board. We met for a brief worship service on the mess deck in the evening after chow but, since many of the men were on duty, attendance was sparse.

Sometime after breakfast the next day, the "holy helo" returned and I bid a hasty farewell to the officers and crew of this venerable destroyer. She had survived combat during World War II and the Korean War, and was continuing to provide fire support off the coast of South Vietnam. She would soon depart to take part in a SEATO (South East Asia Treaty Organization) exercise called Sea Spirit. I was privileged to have had this brief moment walking her decks.

I enjoyed another routine pick-up by the "holy helo." The harness was lowered and attached to the cable; I secured myself in the harness and gave the signal to start the winch. Waving to the sailors below, I enjoyed the moment swinging in the wind suspended above the sea. With a little help getting through the hatch, I was soon aboard the chopper returning to my home away from home. As I viewed the receding destroyer from my perch in the helicopter, little did I know she was a doomed ship. I may well have been the last chaplain that many of her crew ever saw or heard.

Back on the OKI-3, the Marines were still engaged in the Tet Counteroffensive. The USS Okinawa was nearing the end of her eight-month deployment and the hospital ward was reaching full capacity with recovering wounded. Despite their wounds, the Marines had survived and would soon be on their way home. Overall, the mood in the ward was almost jovial.

Our involvement in the Tet/69 counteroffensive ended on May 27, 1969. Our "guests" were debarked and the Marines of SLF Alpha were all off-loaded. BLT 2/26, Marine Medium Helicopter Squadron 362, the Navy medical teams and the wounded all had departed. It was announced that we were going home via an R & R port call in Hong Kong. Even though everyone was eager to return home, the prospect of five days in exotic Hong Kong was not an unwelcome delay.

After our five-day sightseeing and shopping spree, we were back aboard the OKI-3 for one final command function. The other four ships that were part of Amphibious Squadron Five were also in Hong Kong. Admiral John S. McCain, Jr. (Senator John McCain's father), Commander-in-Chief of the Pacific Fleet, wanted to visit the Squadron before we departed. The five ships were aligned in formation for the admiral. He came aboard the OKI-3 and spoke to the officers and crew, thanking us for our service. Following the admiral's visit we broke formation and headed for home.

The OKI-3 message center received shocking news shortly after we sailed from Hong Kong. The terse, horrifying message was: "The USS Frank E. Evans has been cut in two following a collision with HMAS Melbourne, an Australian aircraft carrier, during a night training exercise on June 3, 1969. The severed bow sank immediately with a loss of seventy-four lives. An investigation is underway."

That was the gist of information radioed to us. It would be some time before the investigation was completed and I would learn more of the devastating details. As it turned out, an inexperienced junior officer on the deck of the USS Evans had tragically ordered a wrong turn into the path of the Aussie carrier. The skipper of the HMAS Melbourne was cleared of any wrong-doing.

I can scarcely describe the emotions that churned within me as I digested the horrifying news. I had ministered aboard the USS Evans only a few weeks previously and knew that I may have talked to some of the men that went down with the bow of the ill-fated ship. What more could I have said or done to prepare them for eternity? I grieved for the lost men and for their families.

Once again I was reminded of the uncertainties of life. Had I done everything possible to secure my family's well-being should something happen to me? Thank God, they had a large, loving support group of family and church. And always in the back of my mind was the nagging reminder that when I returned I had to get things squared away with my church. Life was too uncertain to leave loose ends unattended. I must be sure to indicate my variance with Assemblies of God doctrine. To do so might end my chaplaincy career, but that was a risk I must take.

In less than three weeks the OKI-3 would be back to her home port in San Diego. She was scheduled to enter dry dock in Long Beach for overhaul soon after our return. After our over-haul was completed we would have to undergo sea trials and training exercises in preparation for our next WestPac cruise to Vietnam. Our sailing date was set for May, 1970. The next annual questionnaire for credential renewal would likely arrive in December, 1969 so there was plenty of time to get the doctrinal issue resolved before the next cruise. Would I still be a Navy chaplain when my ship left San Diego?

The Holy Spirit had nudged my conscience concerning being honest with my church about the issue of tongues while I was in Vietnam. That was the issue which I determined to settle when I returned home. I do not address this issue as a professional scholar or academic. I come as a student of Scripture seeking truth and trying to conform my life to truth as the Spirit illuminates my mind and heart. I want to respond to truth no matter how painful that may be initially because I know it will always lead me closer to Jesus Christ who is Truth. I cannot deny, however, that I still struggle when a new truth emerges, or an old one long ignored is aroused, and demands a response. It is not easy for me to leave my comfort zone, nor will it be for some of you as we continue our journey.

CHAPTER 6

MUST SPIRIT BAPTISM BE
INITIALLY EVIDENCED BY TONGUES?

Disagreement on this next critical issue put me in the cross-hairs of
ardent denominational traditionalists. The traditionalists were
convinced that the slightest deviation from the traditional stance
about speaking in tongues should not be tolerated. Fortunately for
me, there were gracious and spiritually astute men in places of
authority who pleaded my cause when necessary. Even so, there
were times when my future with my church was uncertain. I shall
share some of my journey with you; it's been quite a ride.

DIALOGUE WITH THE ROCKY MOUNTAIN DISTRICT

In December of 1969, a few months after returning from Vietnam,
I received the annual credential renewal questionnaire sent to all
Assemblies of God ministers. At that time I still belonged to the
Rocky Mountain District where I had been ordained in 1958. It
was customary for the District to forward the completed form to
national headquarters in Springfield, Missouri.

The District could indicate a recommendation of "approval" or
"disapproval," but it was up to the national headquarters to make
the final determination whether credentials would be granted.
Nevertheless, District input was taken seriously and often
followed.

THE CRITICAL QUESTION

When I received the credential renewal form I didn't have to
struggle with my reply to the one question that was critical. I had
fought that battle already while in Vietnam. The question was this:
"Do you fully subscribe to the Statement of Fundamental Truths as
contained in the General Council Constitution Article V?"

I indicated that I did not fully subscribe to this statement: "The
baptism of believers in the Holy Spirit is witnessed by the initial
physical sign of speaking with other tongues as the Spirit of God
gives them utterance." (Acts 2:4) I attached an explanation of my

basis for disagreement.

Making a break with the religious tradition in which I had been reared was not easy nor painless. I knew both from Scripture and experience that the supernatural gifts of the Holy Spirit were still operative in the Church. But I could find no substantive Scriptural support for our doctrinal insistence that there could be no valid Spirit baptism that was not initially evidenced by speaking in tongues.

WOULD MY CREDENTIALS BE RENEWED?

In February, 1970, I received a letter from the Secretary-Treasurer of the Rocky Mountain District, a fine man but very conservative and legalistic in his approach to Assemblies of God doctrine. He wrote that the District Presbytery had met and they had decided that they could not endorse my credential renewal form. Since the District did not have the authority to refuse my credentials he included the paragraphs below:

"The brethren further decided that your questionnaire, together with your attached statement, should be sent to the General Council office, and should be referred to the General Council Executive Presbytery for their decision and disposition of the matter, inasmuch as you are also an Assemblies of God chaplain under appointment by the Assemblies of God. It was felt by our District Presbytery that the General Council Executive Presbytery should make an interpretation and decision regarding your credentials, in view of this position and in view of your statement which you attached to your application for renewal of your fellowship card.

"I am therefore writing, Brother Brown, to mention that the final decision will rest with the General Council Executive Presbytery, and until we receive some final word from them, there will be a delay in any action which may be taken in regards to your credential renewal. As soon as we receive word from the General Council, we will let you know what their decision is regarding this matter."

While I was in limbo awaiting a decision from the denominational leaders in Springfield, I wrote several letters fleshing out my position. I wrote to the Reverend Ted Gannon,

72

Chairman of the Assemblies of God Commission on Chaplains, and concluded one of my letters to him with this paragraph:

"When dogma is logically and exegetically warranted, I can be as dogmatic as the next man. It is very difficult for me to be dogmatic on the basis of an inference or an assumption. An assumption that is recognized as an assumption is one thing but to construct a dogma upon an assumption is to build upon theological quicksand. I think we may be afraid to be theologically forthright at this point lest we undermine our Pentecostal uniqueness. I am convinced this is a false fear."

Over the years I had become friends with Thomas Zimmerman, General Superintendent of the Assemblies of God. I wrote him at some length, dealing not only with the doctrinal issue but also sharing some of my frustration. After all, he was my senior pastor. Here are excerpts from one letter:

"I would be less than candid if I failed to acknowledge that I am hurt by what is transpiring. Not the least of the hurt is that brothers can be isolated from one another over issues that have nothing to do with the heart of the gospel. What a cycle. A few decades ago the Pentecostal believers were anathema to the old-line denominations. Denominational traditions were so inflexible that there was no place for Christians who emphasized the baptism in the Holy Spirit, speaking in tongues, and all the other charismatic ministries of the Holy Spirit. The 'traditions of the elders' forced us to establish new fellowship groups which developed into a variety of Pentecostal denominations. Now our own traditions have become inflexible and we have come full circle. Thank God, the Holy Spirit is not limited to the boxes we build and try to confine Him in.

"There are other aspects of this situation that hurt me, also. Sure, I'm worried about some of the possible effects upon my ministry in the naval chaplaincy. . . But what can I do? Should I hold mental reservations but fail to reveal them? I have reason to believe that others share my convictions but have not so stated. I can well understand their reluctance and have not the slightest inclination to judge them. I have a full-time job passing judgment on my own motives and actions.

"Despite a certain amount of apprehension which I feel from time to time, the Lord has given me a great deal of peace about the

ultimate outcome of this matter. Donna is a real princess about the whole thing, but naturally I am concerned about the future as it relates to my family. Should the Executive Presbytery decide that my credentials will not be renewed, I would greatly appreciate some reasonable length of time be allowed whereby I could affect a transfer into another denomination. Would this be considered or is it asking too much?"

I received only a noncommittal response from the General Superintendent.

FURTHER BUREAUCRATIC DELIBERATION

I wrote a detailed letter to the Presbytery Board of the Rocky Mountain District so as to leave no room for misunderstanding my position. I had covered all the bases within my denomination but there was one more letter I needed to write. My senior chaplain suggested I write Rear Admiral James Kelly, Chief of Navy Chaplains, and acquaint him with all that was going on with my denomination.

I knew Chaplain Kelly, as he had visited the USS Okinawa when we were operating off the coast of Vietnam. In fact, he had preached for me on Christmas Day, 1968. He was a Southern Baptist and not unfamiliar with the Assemblies of God. I enclosed with my letter all the correspondence which had taken place between me and the various denominational officials. I told him that if I couldn't continue within the fellowship of the Assemblies of God, I would seek to affiliate with another endorsing agency so that I could continue serving as a chaplain.

The correspondence continued on into April without any final resolution. The last week of April, 1970, I received a letter from the Rocky Mountain District Secretary stating that the General Council Executive Presbytery had recommended that I be given provisional credential renewal *"until such time as you return from sea duty and the General Council brethren would have an opportunity for consultation with you in regards to your belief on this particular statement of fundamental truths."* He further stated that the District Presbytery would meet the first week of May and make a determination as to what disposition they would recommend to the General Presbytery. Well, provisional renewal was better than none at all.

On May 1, 1970, the USS Okinawa departed once again to WestPac and I was still aboard as chaplain. This would be a short cruise for me since my two-year assignment to sea duty would conclude in early July and I would fly home from somewhere in the Pacific.

As it turned out, my last cruise on the OKI-3 was almost like a vacation cruise. Our flight deck was loaded with tied-down fighter planes we were delivering to New Zealand. On the way to New Zealand, we crossed the equator and I got initiated into King Neptune's kingdom. Somewhere out in the middle of the vast South Pacific we were overtaken by a fierce typhoon. It did some minor damage to our superstructure but all the fighters on deck came through intact.

Our port call for a week in New Zealand was wonderful. I met some great people, including the pastor of an Assemblies of God church. The Royal New Zealand Navy treated us splendidly, including hosting a fabulous dinner full of pomp and ceremony. I arranged bus tours for our crew to enjoy the scenic beauty of the North Island. I would love to return someday to visit again this beautiful land and gracious people.

From New Zealand we sailed to Sasebo, Japan, where the OKI-3 was to undergo some repair in the naval repair facility there. It was here that my replacement came aboard and I said good-bye to my friends and shipmates. After being relieved I had a couple of days in Japan before my flight to California. There was a World Fair going on in Osaka, so I took the train to the site and spent a day touring the exhibits. I went from Osaka to the U.S. Air Base at Yokota and secured a room in officers' transient quarters, and then flew nonstop from Yokota to March Air Force Base near Riverside, California. Donna and Celia met me there and we drove back to San Diego, happy to be together again.

MY PRESENTATION TO THE DISTRICT OFFICIALS

Shortly after arriving home, I received notification that the Rocky Mountain District officials wanted to meet with me and the Reverend Ted Gannon, Chairman of our Chaplains Commission, as soon as possible. Donna's and my parents lived in Colorado and we planned to visit them before reporting to my new duty station. Ted Gannon was to fly into the Denver airport and the officials and I would meet him there in one of the conference rooms.

I had prepared a written statement which I intended to read so as not to misspeak. I was sure each word would be scrutinized and parsed by the District officials. At the appropriate time I read my statement and I could tell by the looks on the faces of the Coloradans that they were not pleased. I quoted from Carl Brumback, a well-known Assemblies of God author whose book *What Meaneth This* was a defense of the Assemblies of God's position on tongues. Brumback had quoted approvingly Charles G. Finney's preface to his Systematic Theology. I read to them the quote from Finney, a portion of which I include here:

"A Christian profession implies the profession of candor and of disposition to know and obey all truth. It must follow, that Christian consistency implies continued investigation and change of views and practice corresponding with increased knowledge. No Christian, therefore, and no theologian should be afraid to change his views, his language, or his practices in conformity with increasing light."

This quote apparently hit a raw nerve. The District officials were definitely not interested in any "continued investigation and change of views" relating to increased knowledge. They were fiercely opposed to the mild change of view that I represented. They were traditionalists to the core and nothing could change their traditional interpretation about tongues. Seeing what was transpiring, Ted Gannon spoke up in my defense. He indicated that my view might be acceptable if interpreted a certain way. I wasn't sure I completely agreed with his interpretation, but this was no time to quibble.

I realized what Ted Gannon had done. As an Assistant General Superintendent, he had "pulled rank" on the District officials who had wanted to deprive him of one of his chaplains. He did it in a very gracious manner and made sure the officials were extolled for their excellent work in the Rocky Mountain District. But the bottom line was that I was granted my credential renewal for the remainder of 1970. However, I knew the District officials were not pleased and that I would have to run through their gauntlet again for my 1971 credential renewal.

A WELCOME INVITATION TO TRANSFER

On the Chaplains' Commission which Ted Gannon chaired sat a senior Army chaplain, Colonel John Lindvall. John was a friend whom I had known for many years and he had become aware of my struggle for credential renewal. He contacted me and said I should speak to a good friend of his who had been an Assemblies of God U.S. Army chaplain during World War II. His name was Joe Gerhart and he was currently District Superintendent of the Northern California/Nevada District of the Assemblies of God. John was senior chaplain at Sandia Army Base near Albuquerque, New Mexico, where Donna's brother, Lanny Wirth, lived. Providentially, Joe Gerhart was visiting John in Albuquerque at the same time we planned to visit Lanny. Since our visits overlapped, John made arrangements for Joe and me to get together.

John, Joe and I met in a restaurant in the "Old Town" section of Albuquerque. I explained my position and told of the opposition to my credential renewal from the Rocky Mountain District officials. Joe Gerhart gave me a big smile and said, "Glenn, transfer into the Northern California/Nevada District. We will have no trouble with your position and we will be glad to have you." What a breath of fresh air that was to my troubled ears. There was light at the end of the tunnel after all.

Donna and I returned to California in August and I reported to the Commanding General of the Marine Corps Supply Depot at Barstow as the assigned Protestant chaplain for his command. In September I wrote a letter requesting that the Secretary-Treasurer of the Rocky Mountain District transfer my pertinent records to the Northern California/Nevada District. I explained that I had informed Joe Gerhart of my request for transfer and was making the request with his approval.

TRANSFER BATTLES

I thought getting this transfer would be a simple administrative procedure. Not so. The Secretary-Treasurer was not going to surrender control of my destiny so easily. He wrote a circuitous reply in which he stated he could not make the transfer without full clearance from the Presbytery. The Presbytery was scheduled to meet the first part of October but the meeting had been canceled. The next meeting was scheduled for early February, 1971, at which time they would consider my request.

It wasn't hard for me to do the math. My current credentials expired January 31, 1971. The Presbyters met in February, 1971. By then my credentials would be expired unless I had them renewed through the Rocky Mountain District and I didn't want to go through that battle again. In his letter denying my request, the District Secretary-Treasurer added this note:

"Our District Superintendent is gone at the present time so I do not have the opportunity to confer with him about your transfer. I will confer with him, however, and will write you again later, as soon as I have some definite direction in regards to sending your transfer of credentials to the Northern California-Nevada District."

I gathered from this he didn't need approval of the Presbyters if the Superintendent approved my transfer.

I did a little research into the Rocky Mountain District constitution and found this gem: *"A certificate of transfer shall be issued to all workers leaving the District to permanently locate in another district. . . ."* (Art. IX, Sect. 4) Using this as ammunition, I sent a reply to Colorado:

"In view of the action taken by Springfield; in view of my geographical absence from the Rocky Mountain District; in view of my own desire to associate with the Northern California/Nevada District Council; and in view of the instructions in the Rocky Mountain District Constitution and Bylaws, I respectfully request that you reconsider your decision so as to make possible that a certificate of transfer be issued without further delay."

I wrote another letter to the Superintendent of the Rocky Mountain District requesting that he approve my transfer and appended a copy of the letter I had sent the Secretary-Treasurer.

It was now mid-October. I thought I had crossed every "t" and dotted each "i" but apparently not. Another reason suddenly surfaced which made it impossible to effect the transfer. Barstow was in Southern California and policy would not permit me to be transferred to a District outside my geographical region. Bartlett Peterson, the General Secretary, was cited as the authority for this ruling.

I quickly wrote the General Secretary:

"I realize that generally one's locale of ministry determines which District has credential jurisdiction. However, in all of my ministry in the chaplaincy, I have never been stationed in Colorado, so obviously an exception to the general rule is made for military chaplains. Otherwise, I would have had to transfer my credentials numerous times since I have served in various Districts for lengthy periods of time.

"Having established that a general rule has been waived, I am desirous of knowing who in the General Council has authority to approve such a waiver. I desire to petition for waiver to transfer to the Northern California/Nevada District Council even though I am temporarily stationed in Southern California."

I then listed four positive reasons why the transfer should be approved. I indicated I was sending a copy of the letter to each District concerned as well as to the Chairman of the Chaplains Commission.

It was now mid-November. Apparently I got the General Secretary's attention, because a short time later my transfer was approved and acted upon.

At my earliest opportunity I paid a courtesy visit to the Northern California/Nevada District headquarters in Santa Cruz. I was delighted to see Joe Gerhart again and meet Bill Vickery, the District's Secretary-Treasurer. I assumed that Joe had shared with his Secretary-Treasurer my stance so I needn't go over that plowed ground for the foreseeable future. I loved the chaplaincy ministry I had been called to. God is good!

A TRAUMATIC BETRAYAL

Things continued to go well in my ministry. During my first year at Barstow, I was promoted to full Commander. At the completion of my tour in Barstow in 1973, I was selected to attend the "Senior Course" for Navy chaplains. This was a course to prepare Commanders for greater responsibility and administrative skills they would need, especially if promoted to Captain. Following Senior Course I was assigned as senior chaplain for Camp Hansen, Okinawa, on the staff of Colonel Al Gray, Camp and Regimental Commander. Camp Hansen was the largest Marine base outside the United States, with eight chaplains assigned. Colonel Gray was promoted rapidly after our tour together. As a four-star General he was selected to be Commandant of the Marine Corps in 1987. He was a great Commanding Officer and it was a privilege to serve on his staff.

After completing my unaccompanied tour in Okinawa, I was assigned a dream assignment as senior Protestant chaplain at Moffett Naval Air Station in Mountain View, California.

There was a lovely historical chapel with paid musical staff of choir director and organist. The chapel congregation was comprised of both active duty personnel and military retirees who lived in the area. I looked forward to three good years at Moffett but it was not to be. One of the most traumatic events of my life was about to unfold. I'll share that briefly before I continue with my doctrinal dispute with the Assemblies of God.

The senior chaplain at Moffett was a Roman Catholic priest. We were both Commanders but because he had been passed over for promotion, he had more years in grade than I. He was a rather surly, unfriendly fellow but I didn't think much of it. After a year and a half at Moffett, I was up for promotion to Captain. I fully expected to be selected, and with good reason, in view of the schools the Navy had sent me to and my regular Navy status. I also knew that Colonel Gray had rated me in the top one percent of chaplains with a strong recommendation for swift promotion. You can imagine my consternation when the promotion list was published in July, 1977 and my name was not included.

Promotion boards depend on the "fitness reports" that are submitted annually on each officer. I never paid much attention to my report unless the Commanding Officer brought it to my attention. Only a bad fitness report could account for my failing promotion, so I requested to see my last report and was dismayed at what I saw.

Not only did I see the report but also the worksheet submitted by the senior chaplain that guided the skipper in making his marks. The worksheet was filled with falsehoods and misrepresentations. I went immediately to the skipper, who was about to retire, and told him what his senior chaplain had done. Essentially, he had committed perjury on an official document. Most of his false statements and accusations easily could be refuted and I soon had a document on the C.O.'s desk that clearly pinpointed the discrepancies. In addition, I included a "brag sheet" that highlighted positive accomplishments produced on my "watch." He reviewed it and promised to rectify the serious error and send in a corrected fitness report. The Catholic priest had requested retirement and both he and the C.O. were scheduled to depart about the same time. I was fighting a battle with my emotions regarding what he had done. What was his purpose? I was confident that with the corrected report, I would be promoted next year. No use crying over spilled milk. God was still in control. All I could do was commit it to the Lord and get on with my ministry.

As I sat in my office a few weeks later, there was a knock on the door and the retiring Catholic priest entered my office and stood before me. He said he must talk to me. I invited him to sit but he insisted on standing as a shocking story unfolded.

"Glenn, years ago I was up for promotion to Captain. My senior chaplain, a Protestant, recommended a fitness report that prevented me from being promoted. I vowed that if I ever got a chance to take revenge on a Protestant, I would do it. You were my chance and I got even at your expense."

I just looked at him and there were tears in his eyes as he continued, "Glenn, can you forgive me?" His voice broke as he spoke. It is hard for me to describe the miracle that God did in my heart at that moment. You would have to know the depth of my disappointment and the hurt produced by this man before you could begin to grasp the immensity of the miracle. I am, by nature, very competitive. I had planned to enter the athletic world before God called me into the ministry. I've softened over the years but I still don't like losing, not even to my grandchildren. I had every reason to believe that I would be promoted to Captain, which is the top of the promotion ladder for Navy chaplains unless one is selected for Chief of Chaplains or Deputy Chief. This man had deliberately torpedoed my dream, and my pride, my ego, my old nature demanded retribution.

GOD'S SUPERNATURAL GIFT OF FORGIVENESS

When I saw the tears and sensed the genuineness of the priest's repentance, a spirit of acceptance and forgiveness swept over me.

God's Spirit was providing power I didn't possess. I arose from my chair, took Joe in my arms and we wept together. The Spirit of God was in that office and removed every desire for revenge or retribution.

Another miracle was unfolding before my eyes. This Catholic priest whom I considered a renegade perjurer masquerading as a man of God was standing before me, confessing his dastardly deed, and asking my forgiveness. I would never in a hundred years have thought it possible. But here he was in my arms shedding tears of repentance, begging me to forgive him.

The same Holy Spirit that had melted my heart had produced a miracle of confession and repentance in the soul of this Catholic chaplain. How could I ever again doubt the power of God to do the humanly impossible? I had witnessed a double miracle that was at least as supernatural as restoring the dead to life. None but God could have accomplished it.

A CHOICE BETWEEN JUSTICE AND MERCY

Following the experience in my office, I was faced with a moral dilemma. If I continued in the Navy and received the promotion I so ardently desired, and for which the Navy had prepared me, it would be necessary to reveal the criminal action of my Catholic colleague in falsifying an official document.

I knew that the experience in my office was a holy moment. Should I tarnish my colleague's confession and repentance by sharing it so as to advance my own career? I was only forty-nine and could continue serving as a Navy chaplain for another fifteen years. I wrestled with these issues. Whatever I did would not hurt his career, since he had now retired.

However, I came to the conclusion that I would rather err on the side of hurting myself than hurting a brother. I made a decision (I still am not sure it was the right one) to resign from active duty. A friend in the Chief of Chaplains' office called, trying to persuade me not to leave the chaplaincy. Rightly or wrongly, I felt I shouldn't tell him any details concerning why I was resigning.

With my eight years' previous service in the Army and Air Force, I retired from the Navy with twenty-six years of accumulated service. Friends and Navy officials came to honor me and my family in my retirement ceremony on December 30, 1977. I left, still torn by the question as to whether or not I had made the right decision. If it was a mistake, I knew God can use even our human errors to work for good. I placed my past and future firmly in His hands.

I have already related pertinent events that took place during my nearly fourteen years as Senior Pastor at the Assemblies of God Church in California. Donna and I were privileged to invest that time with some wonderful people who enriched our lives, and continue to do so.

Now let's fast forward several years.

CONTINUED DOCTRINAL STRUGGLES WITH THE ASSEMBLIES OF GOD

My last Sunday as pastor was November 25, 1991, and at the start of the new year I filled out the annual questionnaire for credential renewal. Twenty-two years had elapsed since I had first shared my variance with Assemblies of God doctrine regarding speaking in tongues. During that time I didn't always reiterate my differences on the form. Rather, I either just checked "yes" or added a note, "Except as previously noted and discussed."

But as I filled out the renewal form for 1992, I realized I was entering a new phase of my ministry, although I wasn't yet sure just where God would call Donna and me. I was sixty-four years old and in good health, ready for whatever God had in mind.

There were new officials both in the National Office and District Office since I had accepted the invitation to transfer into Northern California/Nevada District, so I thought it best to be transparent and stir the waters once again. I checked "no" on the question, "Do you fully subscribe to the Statement of Fundamental Truths as contained in the General Council Constitution Article V?" I was then required to submit an explanatory statement defining my differing view, so I submitted essentially the same statement that I had given more than twenty years previously.

My form was forwarded to national headquarters and received a quick response from Joseph R. Flower, the General Secretary. His father had been one of the founders of the Assemblies of God and "Flower" is a hallowed name in our history. The Secretary very graciously sent me a detailed six-page letter reiterating the Assemblies of God position. I knew the position quite well; in fact, I used some of his very statements to support my variance with the traditional position. The Reverend Flower concluded his letter with this statement:

"Chaplain Brown....I would sincerely hope that you might come to an unqualified commitment to the Assemblies of God position relative to the manifestation of speaking with tongues as the scriptural evidence of the Spirit's baptism/ filling. It really is not appropriate for an Assemblies of God minister to take any other position. I do appreciate your openness in this matter and desire to not be contentious."

He added this P.S.:

"We will hold up on your renewal until you have had an opportunity to take a deeper look at your position.

"We would like a more positive statement of your commitment to our Assemblies of God position."

Part of my reply to the General Secretary is as follows:

"Dear Brother Flower,

"While I am a Pentecostal Christian, I am also a Christian in the larger context of the universal church. As an honest exegete of Scripture, I must acknowledge that our dogma concerning tongues as the absolutely required initial physical evidence of the baptism in the Holy Spirit is built on a certain degree of assumption rather than the categorical teaching of Scripture. You, of course, are aware of that.

"In writing to me of the Apostle Paul's experience you stated, 'It is reasonable to assume that he began to speak with tongues when he was first filled with the Spirit.' Likewise, you note concerning the experience of the Corinthian church, 'Furthermore, though no mention is made in Acts 18:1-17 of the Corinthian converts speaking in tongues or even being filled with the Spirit during Paul's ministry there, yet in the light of Paul's corrective teaching to them in 1 Corinthians chapters 12-14, it is reasonable to assume that was when they were first filled with the Spirit and began to speak in tongues.'

"I certainly agree with your assumptions but because they are assumptions and not the unequivocal declarations of Scripture, I cannot be dogmatic where Scripture is not. I am uncomfortable

with a position that puts God in a box He has not unequivocally defined for Himself. To say that one who has not spoken in tongues has not been baptized in the Holy Spirit places a limit on the Baptizer that He does not clearly place on Himself. Consequently, neither can I, in good conscience, attempt to limit His sovereignty.

"I think I have explained my position as clearly as I can. If my statement is incompatible with our Pentecostal position, then I will accept whatever decision my brethren reach as far as my credential renewal is concerned. I have reason to believe that many in our movement share my position. I do not see my stance as weakening our Pentecostal testimony but rather giving it a much more solid biblical base."

The letter above, written February 18, 1992, included copies to my good friend Donald Annas, the Northern California/Nevada District Superintendent and Richard Hopping, District Secretary-Treasurer.

I included this note to Don Annas:

"Dear Don, Again, let me reiterate. I don't want you caught in the middle. If Springfield doesn't want to renew my credentials then I am sure the Lord will direct me to another credentialing agency."

On his own initiative, but with my deep appreciation, Superintendent Don Annas wrote a personal letter to the Reverend Flower. He spoke very warmly of my history of ministry within his District and included pertinent documents dating back to 1970 when I had transferred into the Northern California/Nevada District. He concluded his letter with a request that my credentials be renewed. I never received any more correspondence from the General Secretary but very soon my fellowship card arrived in the mail. District Superintendents do have some clout.

THE DEFINITIVE SCRIPTURAL ANSWER

I must now return to the task at hand which is to more definitively deal with this question: Must the baptism in the Holy Spirit be initially evidenced by speaking in tongues? I believe the answer to this question is a resounding "NO" for at least these reasons: The Pentecostal tradition of evidential tongues has no foundation in Scripture. It is a hallowed tradition untouched by sufficient exegesis or scriptural research.

1) It can and has at times led to a spiritual caste system. This is not of God.

2) It is based upon a series of illogical and fallible assumptions.

3) It has resulted in multiple abuses which the scripturally assigned purpose of tongues would have prevented.

4) Most grievously, it elevates an erroneous tradition into a major doctrine that creates a giant barrier to the fulfillment of Christ's prayer for unity among his followers.

I became thoroughly convinced that there was no scriptural support for insisting that speaking in tongues must accompany every valid Spirit baptism. I searched diligently to find a text upon which to base this teaching. I read the books, articles and sermons of those who espoused this tradition. The text used again and again as proof of this divisive dogma is Acts 2:4. *All of them were filled with the Holy Spirit and began to speak in other tongues as the Spirit enabled them.*" (NIV) This tells us the historical fact of *what* happened but doesn't give a clue as to *why* it happened. It says nothing about the *purpose* of the Spirit inspired languages spoken at Pentecost and subsequently. "What does this mean?" was the cry of the Jewish pilgrims. "*This*" obviously refers to the languages supernaturally spoken by the disciples which so amazed the onlookers. I prayed for guidance as I pursued an answer to this question: "If speaking in tongues is not intended to be the initial physical evidence of Spirit baptism, what is the purpose?"

Throughout the course of my search, new insights began to emerge. I knew all along that the answer must lie in Scripture. I finally realized the only Scripture the first apostles had was the Old Testament. Was the answer in the Hebrew Scriptures? Indeed it was! Eventually I saw truths so obvious I was astounded I had overlooked them. I had read them multiple times without seeing their significance. Was I blinded, like Peter, by religious tradition? As I related the Old Testament passages to the historical record in the New Testament I saw both a reasonable and scriptural purpose for tongues. My appreciation for this linguistic gift increased rather than diminished. As the truth of Scripture released me from the shackles which my own Pentecostal tradition had bound me, I had a wonderful sense of release. Let me lead you through the familiar

Scriptures that suddenly became living coals that burnt the scales from my spiritual eyes.

CHAPTER 7

A SCRIPTURAL AND REASONABLE PURPOSE FOR GIFT OF TONGUES

Speaking in tongues was never meant to be the unique initial evidence of the baptism in the Holy Spirit. Among American Pentecostals it has become a hardened tradition supported by an extensive denominational bureaucracy. I shared this dogma for years until I finally realized it was just a hallowed tradition based upon assumptions and not a definitive doctrine of Scripture. A doctrine so divisive should be absolutely, unequivocally taught in Scripture in order to be accepted by Bible believing Christians. One thing we do know for sure; this dogma is notoriously divisive. If it is not true, we Pentecostals who advance this tradition must answer to Christ for thwarting the answer to His prayer for unity amongst His followers (John 17). Our tradition, founded on assumptions, has built an impenetrable wall between brothers and that wall must eventually come down.

At three places where the Holy Spirit was outpoured (Jerusalem, Caesarea, and Ephesus), Scripture specifically states that the recipients spoke in tongues. From this fact, most American Pentecostals have drawn the conclusion that God will not baptize in the Spirit without providing the initial physical evidence of tongues. There are two additional instances (Samaria and Saul in Damascus) where nothing is said about speaking in tongues at Spirit baptism. Pentecostals assume that the Samaritans and Saul spoke in tongues when filled with the Spirit. This may or may not be true.

When I was corresponding with General Secretary Joseph Flower he defended his position by pointing out, "It is reasonable to assume that he (Saul) began to speak in tongues when he was first filled with the Spirit." He makes a similar conclusion concerning the Samaritans. Then, based on these two assumptions, he makes the most flagrant assumption of all: "No one is validly filled with the Holy Spirit unless authenticated by initially speaking in tongues." So a universal is derived from three facts and three assumptions. In logic this is called an inductive fallacy.

Here is a simple example. "I saw three dogs in my back yard that I knew to be German shepherds. I saw two other dogs that looked similar but I couldn't determine their breed. Therefore, all dogs in my back yard must be German shepherds." But what if I went on to say, "And if they are not German shepherds then they are not dogs." You would say, "Absurd." Yes, it is absurd to draw conclusions from unproven assumptions, especially when the conclusions have significant consequences.

To further illustrate, suppose you are a Pentecostal believer defending your position to me, a sincere searcher for spiritual truth. You have declared that no one is baptized in the Holy Spirit unless this experience is initially evidenced by speaking in tongues. I ask you for Scriptural proof and the following dialogue takes place between you (Tom) and me (Glenn):

Tom: Acts 2, Acts 10 and Acts 19 all speak of groups who are filled with the Spirit. Speaking in tongues is indicated as the initial physical response to this experience by all participants.

Glenn: I certainly agree. But what about those accounts where others are filled with the Spirit but there is no mention of tongues?

Tom: You must be referring to the Samaritans' experience and the apostle Paul's experience. I am glad you brought these up. What is your question?

Glenn: For a doctrine as important as the one we are discussing, I want to be assured of the truth. My first question is this: how do you know for certain that the Samaritans and Paul spoke in tongues when they were baptized in the Spirit?

Tom: Well, it is very obvious that they must have done so. They did in the other instances we have discussed. We can safely assume they did so in these two as well.

Glenn: So your conclusion is based on two unproven assumptions. This leads to another question. Is it remotely possible that one or both of your assumptions may not be true?

Tom: No, I don't think it is possible that I am assuming something not true.

Glenn: So you consider yourself free from the possibility of error? You are certainly placing yourself on a higher level than the apostle Peter.

Tom: What do you mean? What's Peter got to do with it?

Glenn: Peter was so captive to his biased Jewish tradition that God had to bombard him with a series of supernatural revelations in order to extricate him from bondage to his religious tradition. Later, he still reverted back to his prejudiced tradition and the apostle Paul rebuked him publicly.

It was Peter's adherence to tradition that won him an even sterner rebuke from Jesus: "Get behind me, Satan" (Mt. 16:23). So let me ask you another question. What if your assumptions are based on human tradition rather than the clear teaching of Scripture? Would you still be so certain of their reliability?

Tom: I refuse to believe that they are not based on Scripture. I think my assumptions are correct.

Glenn: You think. You assume, in other words, that your assumptions are correct. From where do you obtain your certainty? Are you omniscient?

Tom: Of course not. Only God is omniscient. But I still think my assumptions are true.

Glenn: But don't you see? If I am to believe as you believe, I must have more than your assumption that your assumptions are true. Assuming a conclusion based on assumptions is presumption and I can't accept that as a foundation for my life. Since you have admitted that you are not omniscient, is it possible, given only the facts of Scripture, that these believers may not have spoken in tongues when they were filled with the Spirit?

Tom: Well, put like that, I suppose it is remotely possible.

Glenn: Are we sure they were filled with the Spirit?

Tom: Absolutely. You can't question the fact that Scripture makes that plain.

Glenn: No, I can't and I don't want to. All I am trying to do is establish a solid scriptural foundation for my spiritual life. Let me ask you another question. You have finally admitted that your assumptions may not be true. But while we are assuming, let's assume they are true. Is there the possibility that tongues may have had a meaning other than the one your tradition assigns?

Tom: What do you mean? I have never even considered that possibility. Explain it to me.

Glenn: There are two clear, teaching passages of Scripture that help clarify the purpose of tongues. They are both quotes from the Old Testament, the only Bible the apostles had. The first is

Peter's quotation of Joel 2:28-32 in Acts 2:17-21. The second is Paul's loose quotation of Isaiah 28:11-12. The Holy Spirit inspired Peter to quote Joel in answer to the question from the "God-fearing Jews from every nation under heaven." These cosmopolitan travelers saw that those speaking in their various languages were unschooled Galilean peasants. They recognized they were witnessing a supernatural event.

Luke records, "Amazed and perplexed, they asked one another, "What does this mean?" The quotation from Joel is God's answer to their question regarding the "WHY" (purpose) to the "WHAT" (tongues) they had just observed. Joel explains: Tongues signify a whole new era in God's economy of salvation. Tongues (languages) symbolized that all language groups were now eligible to receive the Holy Spirit and salvation without first undergoing Mosaic rites. Gentiles did not have to convert to Judaism to become part of God's chosen people. The universality of the gospel was powerfully symbolized by the various languages supernaturally spoken. Like you, Tom, Peter had difficulty accepting what Joel proclaimed. He was still firmly committed to the ancient tradition of the Jews and it took eight years before he was finally freed in Caesarea.

Paul extracts another clear purpose for tongues from Isaiah. Here is the principle in I Corinthians 14:22: "Tongues, then, are a sign, not for believers but for unbelievers." How could Paul more definitively deny that tongues are meant as a sign or "evidence" to believers? They are meant to signify something to unbelievers.

Tom: Now you have my interest aroused. Can we talk again sometime? I would like to consider the Scriptures you refer to.

As Tom was beginning to realize, an inductive fallacy is not a reliable foundation for a doctrine that denies God ever fills anyone with His Spirit without the initial evidence of tongues. If God intended that to be true He would have clearly revealed it. This doctrine is not based on Scripture but on assumptions that have hardened into an inviolate tradition. We have tried to put God in a box He has not constructed for Himself and He just won't stay confined. Now, let's examine those Scripture passages I spoke about to Tom.

The Scriptures, of course, are the Christian's ultimate guide to truth. The Scripture for the original apostles was the Old Testament. Two apostles, Peter and Paul, quote pertinent passages from the Old Testament which deal with the purpose of tongues at Pentecost and subsequent outpourings.

Although I clearly saw that our tradition had insufficient biblical support, I knew that tongues did accompany Spirit baptism at Pentecost. So what was the purpose of this unique phenomenon? In my search for answers I discovered no one seemed to have asked the question, "Does Scripture reveal a purpose for tongues that clearly refutes the traditional Pentecostal position?" If there is such a purpose, then surely the Bible would not leave this question unanswered. But where was it revealed? I determined to search diligently, praying that the Holy Spirit would lead me into truth. I believe my prayer was answered. The prophecy from Joel as quoted by Peter in Acts 2:17-21 came into clear focus. As a Pentecostal preacher I had read this text many times. I had heard sermons preached from it and may have preached a few myself. But I was so shackled by my Pentecostal tradition that I never understood the significance of Joel. Suddenly I saw what I had missed for so many years. How grateful I was to break out of the fog of traditional ambiguity into the light of scriptural assurance.

Have you ever been lost? I guess most people have had the experience of not knowing where they were in relation to where they wanted to be. I've long been amused by the quaint story of the city slicker who took a shortcut to his destination across the back roads of rural Alabama. Having no map, he became hopelessly disoriented and looked for someone to give him directions. He saw a lad leaning against a fence that bordered the dirt road he was traveling. He stopped, got out of the car, and asked the lad, "Boy, can you tell me where I am?" The youngster looked him up and down for a moment, frowning as if in deep thought. Then a smile broke across his face. He pointed his finger in the man's direction and announced triumphantly, "There you is!"

Sometimes we get lost, or at least confused, on our spiritual journey. Fortunately, we have a spiritual road map called the Bible that can help us get back on track. I have been studying this "map" very diligently in an effort to resolve issues that relate to the baptism in the Holy Spirit at Pentecost (Acts 2). For a long time I had clearly seen that my church's traditional interpretation of the

92

purpose of tongues was not solidly based on Scripture. It is crystal clear that tongues did accompany Spirit baptism at Pentecost, Caesarea and Ephesus. The Bible leaves no doubt about that. But why? What was the purpose of the accompanying tongues? As I pondered this question I realized this is exactly the question the Apostle Peter had to wrestle with following the Spirit's outpouring at Pentecost. The thousands of Jewish pilgrims who had come from all over the Roman Empire were thoroughly perplexed by the unexpected sound of their native languages being spoken by unschooled Galileans. They cried out for an explanation. Hearing their demand for an explanation, Peter knew he must reply.

Put yourself in the apostle's shoes. He, along with all the other one hundred and twenty disciples, had just been baptized in the Holy Spirit. It had happened just as John the Baptist had predicted and as Jesus had promised. Nothing in the Baptist's prediction nor in Jesus' instruction had covered the topic of supernaturally speaking in other languages. Peter certainly was no expert. He was a rank beginner on the subject of pneumatology. After all, the Holy Spirit had been outpoured only minutes before.

Peter didn't have a clue as to the meaning of tongues. I believe he breathed an earnest, desperate prayer: "Jesus, You promised that when the Holy Spirit arrived He would lead us into all truth. He is here and I claim Your promise. What shall I tell these thousands of perplexed people? I am also perplexed. Help me, Holy Spirit." NOTE: *If the purpose of tongues was to provide evidence of authentic, valid Spirit baptism, this was the time to make this known. Under the direction of the Holy Spirit, Peter could have announced: "The tongues you heard us speaking are God's sign that we have all been truly baptized in the Holy Spirit. This is the purpose of tongues now and shall continue to be so until Jesus our Messiah returns."*

But, of course, this isn't what happened. Jesus kept His word and the Spirit led Peter to a glorious truth. The apostle was inspired to quote a passage from the prophet Joel. The Old Testament was the authoritative religious "road map" for Jews. Peter's quote from Joel clearly depicts God's purpose for tongues that accompany Spirit baptism. I have no doubt that this text came to Peter by the direct inspiration of the Holy Spirit. The question, "What does this mean?" from the amazed and perplexed multitude was

93

prophetically answered by Joel centuries previously. This prophecy is revolutionary and strikes at the heart of traditional Judaism.

After gaining their attention Peter begins to address the inquisitive throng, *"This is what was spoken by the prophet Joel: 'In the last days, God says, I will pour out my Spirit on all people . . . Everyone who calls on the name of the Lord will be saved.' "* These brief statements summarize the essence of the larger quote.

You may ask, "What is so revolutionary about this?" It may not seem revolutionary to us but the implications of this prophecy turned Peter's world upside down. If you examine the text carefully you will notice that Peter never did comment on or try to explain Joel's words. Joel certainly provides a clear context for the miracle of tongues on that day, showing that the gospel was about to be spread to all nations. So why didn't Peter expound on that prophesy?

There is a good explanation. It's a reason I overlooked for years because I was blinded by my own inherited tradition. *I believe Peter was just not ready, personally and experientially, to understand the full implication of what they were all witnessing.* He was much more familiar and comfortable with the quotation from Psalms, which he quoted next, and which centered on Jesus the Messiah.

Quite frankly, Peter, was still in bondage to his ancient religious tradition that demanded subjection to Mosaic rites for all candidates seeking salvation.

The tenth chapter of Acts dramatically describes how God eventually broke the bars of tradition that imprisoned Peter. Historians estimate the Joppa episode was approximately eight years after Pentecost. Haley indicates it could have been as long as ten years (*Haley's Bible Handbook*, p. 570). During this interval the gospel was not taken to the Gentile world.

Let's do what Peter could not do. Follow along as we examine the text from Joel. The prophet says nothing at all about speaking in tongues. This was the amazing event which aroused the crowd's curiosity and caused them to ask, "What does this mean?" Joel's focus is on the universal outpouring of the Holy Spirit which will characterize the "last days." This is in sharp contrast to the very limited outpouring of the Spirit in previous ages.

Down through the course of Old Testament history prior to

Pentecost the Spirit of God had been active. At various times he had anointed different individuals with gifts for specific service and ministry, primarily prophets within Israel. But never had there been an outpouring of the Spirit upon all humanity. At last the fulfillment of Joel's prophecy was at hand. What the inspired prophet had predicted would signal the beginning of the final age (last days) was actually happening in Jerusalem. Thousands watched and listened in wonder and bewilderment.

What were the signs which Joel predicted would announce the inauguration of the "last days"? They are summed up in the first and last statements quoted by Peter. First, instead of selective outpourings of the Spirit upon a few Israelites there would now be an outpouring on all humanity. There would be no gender barriers, no social, racial or language barriers that would disqualify a person from being eligible to receive the Holy Spirit (Acts 2:17). Second, national origin no longer had a bearing upon salvation. It was no longer limited to Jews or those that converted to Judaism (proselytes). It depended upon each person's response to the gospel. "Everyone who calls on the name of the Lord will be saved." (Acts 2:21)

The line of demarcation between the Old Covenant and the New Covenant was the outpouring of the Holy Spirit at the feast of Pentecost. Joel indicates the numerous national languages supernaturally spoken at Pentecost were the dramatic sign that all language groups were now equally welcome into God's kingdom. From our perspective we can scarcely imagine how revolutionary this concept was for Peter and the other disciples. They could not fully grasp what Joel said.

The sign of "other tongues," pointing to the universality of the gospel, was overshadowed by their bondage to their old, outmoded tradition. Peter couldn't explain Joel's prophecy because he *was not ready for it. He was still emotionally, mentally and spiritually blinded by his biased religious tradition.* At this time in his life, despite spending three years under the teaching of Jesus, he was still convinced that only Jews or proselytes (Gentile converts to Judaism) could be saved. Years later, a series of miracles that began on a roof top in Joppa and ended in Roman army garrison in Caesarea finally broke the shackles of Peter's bondage.

You can read about Peter's emancipation from bondage to his

95

religious tradition in Acts, chapter ten. We will touch upon his experience now and delve into it in greater detail later. It began with a divine "show and tell" display on a house top in Joppa and culminated in the home of a Roman army officer in Caesarea. When Jesus sovereignly poured out His Spirit upon the crude, despised soldiers of the Roman occupation army stationed in Caesarea, Peter's fetters were loosened. Without apostolic sanction, without any previous instruction, without any preconceived ideas relating to baptism in the Holy Spirit, these despised Gentiles began to praise God in languages supernaturally uttered. *The tongues were not only a sign to the Gentiles but to Peter and his Jewish friends.* Bound by their tradition, they did not believe Gentiles were eligible to receive the Holy Spirit or be part of God's kingdom without first converting to Judaism. Caesarea was God's answer to their biased religious elitism.

Peter at last understood the purpose of the tongues spoken at Pentecost. The significance of Joel's prophecy, the relevance of the house top visions in Joppa, and now the surprising outpouring of the Spirit in Caesarea upon Gentiles convinced Peter of the true purpose of tongues. They were the divine sign that no language group, no race and no nationality was to be called unclean or unacceptable into the fellowship of Jesus Christ. Having at last got the message tongues were meant to convey, Peter ordered that these new Spirit-filled believers be baptized in water and welcomed into the infant church.

Before his experience in Caesarea, Peter was like many Pentecostal leaders today. He had been baptized in the Holy Spirit; he was a powerful and successful preacher; he was anointed with multiple gifts of the Spirit including discernment, healing, tongues and miracles (Acts 2-5). Nevertheless, he was absolutely blind to the purpose of tongues which his quote from Joel had clearly revealed. The tentacles of his outmoded and nationalistic religious tradition still clung tenaciously to his mind and heart. As a result, the growth of the church was crippled and the great commission was in jeopardy. It took a series of divine interventions to free Peter from his obsessive bondage.

What will it take to free gifted Pentecostals from their divisive tradition concerning the purpose of tongues? Only God knows, but I believe it must and will happen.

Another pertinent Old Testament passage is quoted loosely by Paul in First Corinthians 14:21. It's from Isaiah 28:11-12. (Paul used examples from the Old Testament era to serve as lessons for the Christian era. He employs Hagar and Sarah, e.g., as symbols of two covenants.) *"In the law it is written; 'Through men of strange tongues and through the lips of foreigners I will speak to this people, but even then they will not listen to me,' says the Lord."* From this Isaiah passage Paul extracts this principle: *"Tongues, then, are a sign, not for believers, but for unbelievers."* (v. 22) The conjunction *"then"* clearly refers back to the Old Testament passage.

Professor Gordon Fee is obviously wrong when he says; "Contrary to many interpretations, this text (v. 22) needs to be understood in the light of what follows, not the other way around." (Fee's 1st Epistle to the Corinthians, p. 681) How a scholar of Fee's stature could reach this conclusion is beyond me (unless he is trying to undergird a tradition to which he is already committed). The reason there are so "many interpretations" contrary to Fee is because his is not supported contextually, theologically nor grammatically. The Greek conjunction *"owste"* will allow no other conclusion.

So what does this mean as it relates to this passage? Obviously, Paul must see a parallel relationship between God's Old Testament chosen people in captivity to the Assyrians who "will not listen" to the sign of tongues (Assyrian language) and His chosen people in the New Testament era who fail to understand the sign of tongues. To conclude otherwise causes the sign of tongues to lose its significance. It is here, I believe, that Fee's interpretation of "sign" misses the whole thrust of Paul's principle given in 1 Corinthians 22. Fee states, "It is a sign that functions to the disadvantage of unbelievers, not to their advantage (*God's Empowering Presence*, p. 241). Not so. The sign of verse 22, if understood, works wondrously to the advantage of unbelievers. Much of the misunderstanding arises because Paul is not just thinking of tongues as manifested in Corinth. He is thinking of tongues in the generic sense as poured out at Pentecost and subsequently. Biblical translator J.B. Phillips is correct when he points out this text doesn't make sense when applied to the Corinthian context. (See note after I Corinthians 14:22 in J.B.

Phillips, *"The N.T. in Modern English".*) But when applied to tongues in the generic sense, the confusion evaporates.

A careful exegetical study will show that the principle in v. 22 does not apply primarily to the Corinthians. It does so only in a secondary sense. Let's examine the facts revealed in Scripture about the three distinct manifestations of tongues at Corinth. We will examine them one by one:

1. DEVOTIONAL TONGUES SPOKEN PRIVATELY IN PRAYER TO GOD (vs. 2)

This is private communication with God, spirit to Spirit, for personal edification. Devotional tongues are not for public display. Consequently, there is no opportunity for unbelievers to receive a "sign" from someone praying in private. Paul's principle obviously does not apply.

2. PUBLIC TONGUES WITH AN INTERPRETATION (vs. 27-28)

If one speaks in tongues publicly there must be an interpretation. If the message is interpreted it is equivalent to prophecy and again the principle does not apply (vs. 5). What if there is no interpreter? Paul's command is brief and pointed. *"If there is no interpreter, the speaker should keep quiet in the church and speak to himself and to God"* (vs. 28).

3. EN MASSE CONGREGATIONAL SPEAKING IN TONGUES (vs. 23)

This is an utterly unacceptable manifestation of tongues by believers gathered for public worship. Paul concludes that if the uninitiated or unbelievers hear this cacophony of confusion, they will conclude the speakers are crazy. So obviously, this is not the sign to unbelievers that Paul has in mind. Furthermore, such en masse speaking is forbidden in verse 27. Since Paul's principle in verse 22 fits none of the manifestations of tongues at Corinth, to whom could this principle apply?

What instances of speaking in tongues are given in the New Testament other than at Corinth? Only the tongues that accompanied the outpouring of the Holy Spirit at Pentecost and subsequently. In these events there is an en masse speaking in tongues fully approved by Jesus Christ, the Baptizer, and by His apostles. Here also, there are unbelievers present who follow the pattern established in the Isaiah text. The "unbelievers" are God's chosen people (Jews) who need a dramatic sign to free them from their captivity to an outmoded religious tradition. Speaking in tongues, which accompanied the Spirit baptisms, fitly represented the momentous grandeur of what God was doing at that point in human history. But Peter missed the sign and was blind to it for years. Tongues were and are a divine signal that every language group, every race, every tribe and nation, indeed, all humanity, are eligible to receive the Holy Spirit and salvation. (Acts 2:17, 21)

As they say, "The proof of the pudding is in the eating." Let's test Paul's principle from Isaiah 28:11-12, applying it to generic tongues and see if it fits. First, consider the initial outpouring of the Spirit at Pentecost. The one-hundred-and-twenty obedient disciples were waiting in Jerusalem for the promised Holy Spirit. John the Baptist had predicted of Jesus, "He will baptize you with the Holy Spirit and fire." When Jesus baptized the disciples He fulfilled John's prophecy and "tongues as of fire" rested on each of them. This was proof, the initial evidence, if you will, that Jesus had baptized them in the Spirit as promised. Tongues were not predicted nor expected. They had no sign value to the disciples. Then why tongues? They were a sign to the unbelievers, just as Paul had declared to the Corinthians: "Tongues are not a sign to believers but to unbelievers."

So who were the unbelievers? There were actually two groups of unbelievers at Pentecost. One group was the biased Jewish disciples who didn't believe Gentiles could enter the Kingdom of God without submitting to the rites of Judaism. We will deal with them later. The primary group was comprised of thousands of Jewish pilgrims from all over the Roman Empire gathered to celebrate the feast of Pentecost in Jerusalem. These did not believe that Jesus was the Messiah. When they heard the unlettered Galilean peasants fluently speaking the native languages of the fifteen nations from which they had gathered, they were flabbergasted.

This supernatural sign attracted their attention. They began to seek an explanation as to the meaning and purpose of this amazing phenomenon. Perplexed, they asked, "What does this mean?" Under the inspiration of the Holy Spirit, Peter quoted from the Prophet Joel. The ancient prophet clearly depicted the meaning and purpose of tongues. A careful reading of Joel's prophecy in Acts

2:17-21 indicates its purpose was to herald and symbolize an epochal transition in God's salvation plan for mankind. But Peter was not ready to accept the revolutionary truth Joel announced. It ran counter to his blinding, binding religious tradition. Therefore he chose another text from which to preach his powerful sermon which led to three thousand conversions.

The sermon text Peter chose was ideally suited for the unbelieving Jewish pilgrims assembled from all over the Roman Empire to celebrate the Feast of Pentecost in Jerusalem. It was a quotation from Psalm 16:8-11 which spoke about the Messiah and His resurrection. Later in his sermon he quoted the first verse of Psalm 110, which speaks of the exaltation of the Messiah. The Holy Spirit powerfully convicted the crowd and they cried out, "Brothers, what shall we do?" Peter's answer is very significant; "Repent and be baptized, every one of you, in the name of Jesus Christ so that your sins may be forgiven. And you will receive the gift of the Holy Spirit." About three-thousand responded. Were they filled with the Holy Spirit? Peter said they would be and I believe they were. Did they speak in other tongues? Apparently not, because other evidence is cited that attests to their being filled with the Spirit.

Scripture is silent but if "evidential tongues" are an essential central teaching for the Church surely it would have been mentioned here. Think how much confusion would have been resolved if Scripture recorded that all three thousand spoke in tongues. The simple fact is: *Tongues were a sign to the three thousand but tongues were not their experience.* Instead, Scripture records a far more significant evidence of the Spirit's presence. *"All the believers were together and had everything in common. Selling their possession and goods, they gave to anyone as he had need. Every day they continued to meet together in the temple courts. They broke bread together in their homes and ate together with glad and sincere hearts, praising God and enjoying favor with all the people. And the Lord added to their number daily those who were being saved."* (Acts 2:44-47)

Let me ask pastors a question. Who would you rather have in your church, a congregation whose chief proof of being Spirit filled is that they all spoke in tongues or a congregation who evidenced Spirit baptism by great generosity, faithful and

100

enthusiastic church attendance, regular meeting in small groups for Christian fellowship and making such a good impression upon the city that many more citizens wanted to join the Christian community? You choose.

Why was it so difficult for the apostle Peter to recognize the meaning of Joel's prophecy? Simply put, it was because of the tenacious grip and blinding power of his religious tradition. For centuries the Jews had lived subject to conditions established under the Old Mosaic Covenant (our Old Testament). For fourteen hundred years the Mosaic covenant established the conditions under which devout Jews lived out their relationship with God. These conditions included circumcision of males, Sabbath observances, strict dietary rules and rigid social separation from other races and people groups. All the disciples baptized in the Spirit at Pentecost were Jews who were born, reared, and thoroughly indoctrinated in the Old Covenant God transmitted through Moses.

Jesus had come to inaugurate a New Covenant sealed by His redemptive blood. It was a covenant of grace and faith rather than of law and works. Unfortunately, all the disciples were exceptionally slow learners regarding the principles of the New Covenant. Although Jesus had clearly taught them about His coming sacrificial death, and although John the Baptist had proclaimed Jesus to be the Lamb of God, the disciples totally discounted all this sacrificial death talk. It didn't fit the traditional view of the Jewish Messiah handed down to them century after century. When it happened as Jesus predicted, it did not break the shackles of their tradition. They simply lost their belief that Jesus was the true Messiah.

Following Jesus' crucifixion they not only lost faith, they lost hope. Terrified that they might also be killed, they went into hiding. Only women followers of Jesus retained their courage. Some of them went to the burial site to anoint Jesus' dead body with perfume and spices. They found the tomb empty and an angel reported He had been raised from the dead. The women reported to the disciples in hiding what they had discovered. The men responded with disdainful unbelief and told the women they were crazy.

The disciples huddled behind locked doors and shuttered

windows, waiting for more time to pass before they slipped away into the darkness. Suddenly the risen Jesus invaded their hiding place. "They were startled and frightened," is Luke's description. They thought they were confronted by a specter up from hades. Jesus quickly put their fears to rest. He invited them to touch and handle Him to confirm His physical body. They were amazed, exuberantly joyful, scarcely daring to believe what they were experiencing. When Jesus suggested they celebrate with a shared meal, their fears left them. Ghosts don't eat.

Jesus saw this as a teachable moment. He gathered the disciples around Him and began to expound the Old Covenant scriptures. From the Scriptures He clearly demonstrated that the New Covenant had been predicted with crystal clarity. Let me quote from Luke's record. *"He said to them, This is what I told you while I was still with you. Everything must be fulfilled that is written about me in the Law of Moses, the Prophets and the Psalms."* Then he opened their minds so they could understand the Scriptures. He told them, *"This is what is written: The Christ will suffer and rise from the dead on the third day, and repentance and remission of sins should be preached in his name among all nations, beginning at Jerusalem. You are witnesses of these things. I am going to send you what my father has promised; but stay in the city until you have been clothed with power from high."* (Luke 24:44-49) This account is astounding in view of what happened during the celebration of the Feast of Pentecost a few weeks later. Oh, the binding, blinding power of errant religious tradition.

Luke continues his historical narrative in the book of Acts. Jesus appeared to His disciples for another forty days after His resurrection. During this time He repeatedly demonstrated that He had indeed defeated death. Although persuaded of the reality of His resurrection, they apparently cannot break free from their tradition of a political, earthly Messianic kingdom. As Jesus bids them farewell before ascending into heaven the disciples ask if He will now restore the kingdom to Israel. He reminds them this is none of their business. The kingdom of God will come in its fullness when the Father decides and not until then. In the meantime they must return to Jerusalem and await the promised Holy Spirit. The Spirit will provide them power to be and do what He has called them to be and do. They are to be His powerful witnesses and they are to take the gospel to the ends of the earth. With these words ringing in their ears, the disciples watch Jesus ascend into the clouds.

The disciples go back to Jerusalem and await the promised Holy Spirit. Ten days later on the day of Pentecost, Jesus pours out the Spirit upon one hundred and twenty expectant disciples. All of this apparently took place in the large upper room where the disciples were assembled. Outside in the temple courtyard, a huge throng of Jewish pilgrims gathered to celebrate the Feast of Pentecost.

After the Spirit fell upon the waiting disciples, they began to joyfully praise God in languages unknown to them as the Spirit enabled them. The disciples knew Jesus had kept His promise because they saw the tongues like fire dancing over the head of each recipient, as John the Baptist had predicted. They left the upper room and began mingling with the celebrating crowd in the temple courtyard. What were unknown languages to the disciples were clearly understood by the celebrating religious pilgrims. They had gathered from many nations all across the Empire. They were astounded to hear Galilean peasants fluently speaking in languages which they recognized as their own national tongues. They cried out in amazement, "How is it we hear uneducated Galileans declaring the wonders of God in our native languages? Will someone please explain what all this means?"

This is where it really gets interesting. Prompted by the Holy Spirit, Peter quoted an explanatory text from the holy writings of the Old Covenant spoken by the prophet Joel. This was not a text Peter had thought about or previously prepared. And if he were going to choose a text on his own, it certainly would not have been the one he quoted under inspiration of the Holy Spirit.

As I have pointed out previously, Peter neither believed nor was ready to practice the text he quoted. Peter preached a great sermon and three-thousand Jews and proselytes were converted. However, he never answered the question, "What is the meaning of these languages spoken by uneducated Galileans?" The answer is contained in Joel's prophecy but Peter neither believed what Joel said nor was he prepared to explain its significance. Consequently he ignored it. Joel's prophecy has to do with the transition from the Old Covenant (Mosaic Law and works) into the New Covenant (grace and faith). Peter was still in bondage to the revered Mosaic tradition.

This is a critical text. We have considered it before but let's consider again the key words of Joel very carefully. *"In the LAST DAYS, God says, I will pour out my SPIRIT on ALL PEOPLE . . . AND EVERYONE who calls on the name of the Lord will be saved."* It's imperative we see the truth that Peter overlooked or ignored. What does Joel mean by *"the last days"*? In its simplest terms, this refers to the final epoch of God's action to win back rebellious mankind before He establishes His eternal kingdom. It encompasses the period of time between the Messiah's redemptive action as the Lamb of God at His first coming and His return to establish His kingdom as the Lion of Judah. It coincides with the period of the New Covenant (Testament) in which we live.

Joel predicts two significant, history-altering changes that will distinguish the New Covenant from the Old Covenant: (1) The Holy Spirit is to be poured out on *all people*. (2) *Everyone* who calls on the Lord will be saved. Of course, the Holy Spirit was present and active in the Old Covenant. However, only a few divinely selected individuals such as prophets, godly kings and anointed musicians were filled with the Spirit. With few exceptions, these were from the nations of Israel or Judah. Under the New Covenant, the old rules are obsolete. Moses is no longer the doorkeeper into God's kingdom. He has been superseded by the Messiah, Jesus Christ, whose sacrificial death atoned for the sins of all mankind. Salvation is no longer linked to national blood lines. The only blood that mattered is the applied blood of the Lamb of God. He is the Door into life eternal.

I trust you can see why Peter found it difficult to try to explain the prophecy of Joel he quoted at Pentecost. He dared not declare that all people could receive the Holy Spirit or that everyone who called on the Lord would be saved. According to his religious tradition, that would be sacrilegious. He was still governed by the traditions of the Old Covenant. The outpouring of the Spirit at Pentecost with the attendant tongues was the line of demarcation between the Old Mosaic Covenant and the New Messianic Covenant. When the crowd of pilgrims asked the meaning of tongues, Peter had no answer. Tongues were as much a surprise to him as to the curious throng. But the Holy Spirit knew the purpose and He inspired Peter to quote the prophet Joel.

Peter's world was being turned upside down and he was not ready to enter the new world. His bondage to Jewish tradition would not permit him to accept the universality of the messianic kingdom. In Peter's mind "all people" and "everyone" referred only to Jews and proselytes (converts to Judaism). He was still convinced that Moses was the gatekeeper through whom one must pass in order to enter Christ's kingdom.

Peter illustrates how enduring and potent are the tentacles of religious tradition. It would take Peter and the other Jewish Christians another eight years to understand what Joel was talking about.

Peter had completely missed what the prophet Joel had predicted about the outpouring of the Holy Spirit at Pentecost. He missed the significance of the "last days" and the ushering in of the New Covenant. He was completely blind to Joel's declaration that tongues pointed to a final era (New Covenant) in which the Holy Spirit would be poured out on all language groups and salvation freely offered to "everyone who calls on the name of the Lord." No longer did Judaism control the door that opened to salvation. For most of a decade he continued in bondage to his Old Covenant tradition. It was the same tradition that caused him to dare resist Christ's revelation of the suffering Messiah. His bondage to tradition brought a stern rebuke from Jesus: "Get behind me, Satan." (Matthew 16:23) Errant religious tradition is one of Satan's favorite snares.

Peter was not ready to consider the implications of Scripture from Joel, revealed to him by the Holy Spirit at Pentecost. But God's dramatic supernatural confrontation in Joppa got his attention and he began to seriously reconsider his theology. However, it was not until he heard the Roman soldiers, fresh out of paganism, begin to praise God in other tongues that his entry into the New Covenant was finally realized. The light of the glorious gospel of Jesus Christ finally penetrated his tradition darkened mind. The "unbeliever" in the universality of the gospel at last became a believer. His response was immediate. Turning to his Jewish Christian companions from Joppa he challenged: "Can anyone keep these people from being baptized with water? They have received the Holy Spirit just as we have. So he ordered that they be baptized in the name of Jesus Christ." (Acts 10:47-48) His patient Lord had finally melted the prideful, obdurate heart of the big fisherman. He was free, free, free to take the gospel to all nations.

He now understood the text he quoted at Pentecost: "In the last days, God says, I will pour out my *Spirit on all people . . . and everyone* who calls on the name of the Lord *will be saved.*" (Acts 2:17, 21)

CONSIDER THE HISTORICAL SIGNIFICANCE OF THIS EVENT

Once again we have a dramatic illustration of the principle Paul draws from Isaiah, "Tongues, then, are a sign, not for believers, but for unbelievers." (1 Corinthians 14:22) Who were the unbelievers at Caesarea for whom tongues were a sign? It is obvious (unless tradition has blinded us) that the sign was for Peter and his brethren from Joppa. They did not believe Gentiles could be saved without submitting to Jewish rites.

Jesus knew it was imperative that His followers recognize the implications of the New Covenant sealed by His blood. They must welcome every language group, every nationality, every race, color and culture into the fellowship of His kingdom. This is BIG, this is transformational. This is what the sign of tongues accompanying Spirit baptism is all about.

This was the purpose at Pentecost, at Caesarea and, yes, at Azusa Street in Los Angeles. To reduce speaking in tongues to individual initial evidence of Spirit baptism for the believer discredits and dishonors its intended purpose and defies Scripture. Rather than promoting spiritual unity and mutual acceptance, it too often becomes divisive and can lead (and has led) to a spiritual caste system. I believe when Pentecostals recognize and proclaim the unifying purpose of tongues that accompany Spirit baptism, Jesus the Baptizer will be honored and the power of the Spirit will be released to unite God's people as never before.

CHAPTER 8

CHRISTIAN UNITY MODELED
WITHIN THE TRINITY

For evangelical Christians, doctrine (hopefully) must be based on the clear teaching of Scripture. If there is disagreement about a particular doctrine, there is a commonly accepted authority that can be researched and investigated. This is not true of tradition. It is based upon experiences (or lack thereof), dogmatic assertions by influential leaders, anecdotal illustrations, and assumptions based largely on isolated texts divorced from the whole context of Scripture. This is true of traditional Pentecostal teaching on tongues. It is just as true for the cessationist tradition that tongues ended when the apostles died or when the canon of Scripture was sealed. When tradition is adopted as a "fundamental truth," this "distinctive" must be protected at all costs. The egos of those in leadership are heavily involved so that any threat to the tradition is taken as a personal threat.

Despite the obstacles to change, I know the Holy Spirit is at work to align Pentecostal tradition with scriptural truth. There is an undercurrent of hunger for life-changing, church-transforming spiritual power devoid of superficiality. This hunger will not be satisfied by initial evidence that can be counterfeited, manipulated and abused. There is a hunger for doctrinal truth that unites the body of Christ instead of a traditional distinctive that fragments the Lord's body. Where are the leaders who will ignite this spiritual hunger into a burning desire for unity firmly founded in truth? I believe God will raise them up when the Church is ready to respond. Lord, speed the day.

If there is any place where absolute spiritual unity is maintained it must be in the heart of the Holy Trinity. Otherwise, the declaration of one God in three Persons becomes meaningless. Jesus experienced this loving unity before the creation of the world, which means before time and space (John 17:24). This is the quality of unity He wanted to bequeath to His followers. In your wildest imagination do you think Jesus would have poured out the Holy Spirit at Pentecost and then introduced a sign (tongues) that would lead to wide-spread disunity within His spiritual family? And if Jesus had devised tongues to provide evidence of valid Spirit baptism, would He not have at least provided a solid scriptural foundation for such a divisive doctrine? Let's take a closer look at why the disunity associated with evidential tongues is a valid basis for rejecting this tradition.

Nowhere in Scripture do heaven and earth come in closer proximity than in Jesus Christ's discourse with His disciples, His family, if you will, during His final Passover celebration. Here we see all the persons of the Trinity, Father, Son and Holy Spirit, on display. We gain a glimpse into the relationship that existed between the Father and Son prior to the creation of the space/time universe. There is even a glimpse into the housing situation in heaven. *"In my Father's dwelling place are many residences. . . ."*

The climax of this remarkable discourse is Jesus' prayer to His Father. The heart of His prayer is contained in this petition: *"I have given them the glory that You gave Me, that they may be one as We are one: I in them and You in Me. May they be brought to complete unity to let the world know that You sent me and have loved them even as You have loved Me."* (John 17:22-23)

A little farther on in His prayer, Jesus speaks of the relationship between Father and Son before the existence of the space/time universe: *"You loved Me before the creation of the world."* (John 17:24) Consider the majestic truths revealed in our Lord's prayer. First consider the existence of the Trinity before creation. Before speaking our space/time universe into being, God existed in the eternal NOW that is associated only with His uniqueness. Can you conceive of someone that has no beginning? I can't. I can imagine it in some sort of science-fiction imagery but I cannot mentally comprehend it. I am time-bound. I can only relate existence to the parameters of time because I have nothing else to relate it to. Now I can conceive of something that has a beginning that continues on and on in an infinite succession of time periods. This is often what people think of when they refer to "eternal" life. But I get bogged down when I wrestle with the concept of a timeless existence that has no beginning.

Theologians have tried to explain God's eternality. Charles Finney, the lawyer-turned-evangelist, offered this explanation: *"Eternity to us means all past, present, and future duration. But to*

God it means only now. Duration and space, as they respect His existence, mean infinitely different things from what they do when they respect our existence. God's existence and His acts, as they respect finite existence, have relation to time and space. But as they respect His own existence, everything is here and now.

"With respect to all finite existences, God can say, 'I was, I am, I shall be, I will do.' But with respect to His own existence, all that He can say is: 'I am, I do.'"

You have a clear understanding of God's eternal being prior to time now, don't you? Of course you don't! Finney himself said, *"Duration and time, as they respect (God's) existence, mean infinitely different things from what they do when they respect our existence."* If His existence is infinitely different from ours then there is no way our finite minds can grasp it.

Not only does God transcend time, He also transcends space. Before God created the "heavens and earth", where did He live? Soloman, the wisest of the wise, grappled with that as he dedicated the temple: *"But will God indeed dwell on the earth? Behold heaven and the highest heaven cannot contain Thee, how much less this house which I have built!"* (I Kings 8:27, KJV)

Although God transcends time and space and is not subject to their natural laws, yet He established those laws and recognizes their relationship to creation. God is not in space in the sense that He is limited by space. But in some sense we might say that space is in God. Space is His invention for finite creatures. Before He created space, where did God exist? God knows but I don't because for me all existence is spatially oriented. We get "spaced out" when we try to visualize this God beyond space.

Jesus refers to another reality about God that boggles my mind. There is God the Father, there is God the Son, there is God the Holy Spirit, but there is but one God. Who can comprehend the Trinity? Neither Jesus, nor anyone else in Scripture, attempts to explain the Trinity. Scripture simply affirms there is one God revealed in the persons of Father, Son and Holy Spirit.

Theologians struggle with this concept. C.S. Lewis was not a theologian but I like his attempt to make the Trinity comprehensible. He writes, *"You know in space you can move in three ways: to left or right, backwards or forwards, up or down. Every direction is either one of these three or a compromise* between them. *They are called the three dimensions. Now notice this. If you are using only one dimension you could draw only a straight line. If you are using two, you could draw a figure, say a square. And a square is made up of four straight lines. Now step further. If you have three dimensions you can build what we call a solid body, say, a cube—a thing like a lump of sugar. And a cube is made up of six squares.*"

Lewis goes on. "*Do you see the point? A world of one dimension would be a straight line. In a two-dimensional world you still get straight lines but many lines make one figure. In a three-dimensional world, you still get figures but many figures make one solid body. In other words, as you advance to more real and more complicated levels, you do not leave behind the things you found on the simpler levels. You still have them, but combined in new ways—in ways you could not imagine if you knew only the simpler levels.*

"*Now the Christian account of God involves just the same principle. The human level is a simple and rather empty level. On the human level one person is one being, and any two persons are two separate beings, just as, in two dimensions (say on a flat sheet of paper) one square is one figure, and any two squares are two separate figures. On the divine level you still find personalities, but up there you find them combined in new ways which we, who do not live on that level, cannot imagine. In God's dimension, so to speak, you find a being who is three persons while remaining one being, just as a cube is six squares while remaining one cube. Of course, we cannot fully conceive of a being like that, just as, if we were so made that we perceived only two dimensions in space, we could never properly imagine a cube. But we can get a sort of faint notion of it. And when we do, we are, for the first time in our lives, getting some positive idea, however faint, of something super-personal—something more than a person. It is something we never could have guessed, and yet, once we have been told, one almost feels one ought to have been able to guess it because it fits in so well with all the things we know already.*" (*Mere Christianity*, p. 138-9)

I am intrigued by Lewis' last statement: "*It is something we never could have guessed, and yet, once we have been told, one almost feels one ought to have been able to guess it because it fits*

110

so well with all the things we know already." What are some of the "things we know already"? Here is one thing we know because Scripture affirms it again and again: *"God is love. Whoever lives in love lives in God, and God in him."* (I John 4:16) Love must have a means of expression to another who can reciprocate or it atrophies. Before God created the space/time universe and peopled it with creatures whom He could love and from whom He could win a love response, there existed a perfect love relationship within the Trinity. Jesus points to this in His prayer: *"You loved Me before the creation of the world."* (John 17:24, NIV)

Within the Trinity there was never any loneliness because Father, Son and Holy Spirit enjoyed perfect harmonious intimate communion and unity (John 17:22). The concept of the Trinity certainly helps us understand God's perfection and completeness prior to creation but it doesn't explain the mystery of the tri-personality of the one God. Are you as amazed and overwhelmed as I am by this awesome divine Being who transcends time and space and exists on a level that we can't comprehend?

Oh, yes, we can know certain things about Him through the things He has designed and made. Paul writes about the revelation of God in nature that is made known to all mankind: *"What may be known about God is plain to them, because God has made it plain to them. For since the creation of the world God's invisible qualities—his eternal power and divine nature—have been clearly seen, being understood from what has been made, so that men are without excuse."* (Romans 1:19-20, NIV)

Just as scrutinizing a work of art can tell us something about the artist's talent and skill, so observing creation can tell us something about God's power and wisdom. But many questions are left unanswered and there is a vast difference between knowing about someone and knowing him.

SO HOW ARE WE TO KNOW GOD?

How are we to comprehend this awesome, transcendent Creator of limitless power and wisdom if we cannot enter His infinite, timeless, spaceless realm? One thing becomes obvious. Since we cannot enter His realm, He will have to enter ours if we are to ever personally know Him. The amazing, astounding, shocking fact is

111

that God has done just that. He has invaded our planet in a way that we could never have imagined.

Here's how an eye-witness describes God's invasion: *"In the beginning was the Word, and the Word was with God and the Word was God. He was with God in the beginning. Through Him all things were made. Without Him nothing was made that has been made. . . . He was in the world and though the world was made through [because of] Him, the world did not recognize Him. . . . The Word became flesh and lived for awhile among us . . . We have seen His glory, the glory of the one and only Son, who came from the Father, full of grace and truth."* (John 1:1-3, 10, 14, NIV)

Here is how St. Paul describes the invasion: *"Who, being in the very nature God, did not consider equality with God something to be grasped, but made Himself nothing, taking the very nature of a servant, being made in human likeness. And being found in appearance as a man, He humbled himself and became obedient to death – even death on a cross."* (Philippians 2:6-8, NIV)

God, in the person of the eternal Son, invaded the stream of humanity at a given point in time and space but the decision to do so was made prior to either. Hear the words of Peter, another eye-witness to the Invader: *"He was chosen before the creation of the world, but was revealed for these last times for your sake. Through Him you believe in God, who raised Him from the dead and glorified Him, and so your faith and hope are in God."* (1 Peter 1: 20-21, NIV)

John states it even more succinctly, *"The Lamb that was slain from the creation of the world."* (Revelation 13:8, NIV) There was always a cross in the mind and heart of the Creator. God knew man would misuse his freedom and assert his rebellious self-will against his Maker. It had been determined in the counsels of heaven that God the eternal Son would divest Himself of His divine glory and come to earth as a human being.

Jesus' mission was two-fold. First, He was to reveal what God was really like in terms that human beings could comprehend and respond to. He was to demonstrate God's love, His compassion, His mercy, His holy character, and His power to break the shackles of sickness, sin and death. Second, the eternal Son, also known as the Logos, the Word, and Immanuel, came to pay the full penalty for man's sin and rebellion by giving His own life as atonement for humanity's evil.

All we will ever know of God's innate character is revealed in Jesus Christ. Ponder the significance of this bold declaration: *"No man has ever seen God, but God the only Begotten [Son], who is at the Father's side, has made Him known."* (John 1:18, NIV) Wow! Did you catch the significance of that? All that can be known about the Triune God who transcends time and space is revealed and explained by the only Begotten Son who invaded space via a mother's womb. The "only Begotten" does not refer to the incarnation wherein Mary was with child by the Holy Spirit. This refers to the eternal relationship within the Trinity in which the life of the Father continually energizes the Son with the same quality of life the Father possesses.

The early disciples struggled with the identity of Jesus. Philip said to Him after three years of observing His life, His supernatural miracles, the raising of Lazarus, and His forgiving sin: *"Lord, show us the Father and that will be enough for us."* Jesus answered, *"Don't you know me, Philip, even after I have been among you such a long time? Anyone who has seen Me has seen the Father. How can you say, 'Show us the Father'? Don't you believe that I am in the Father, and that the Father is in Me?"* Can't you see the wheels spinning in Philip's mind? I can hear his unspoken protest, "But you are a man. How can God be transformed into a human being and still be God?"

I can relate to Philip's confusion. Here's an illustration that helped me. About two hundred miles east of where I live in the state of Washington stands what has been called the Eighth Wonder of the World, the Grand Coulee Dam on the Columbia River. The hydroelectric plant connected with the dam produces a fantastic amount of electric power, as much as six billion, five hundred million watts of surging electrical energy. Imagine plugging your electric razor into that! Before we can "plug in to" that mighty power source, it must be transformed into suitable wattage that conforms to the limitations of our machines. The electricity is not changed into a different kind of energy. It has the same qualities as the vast surge of power that comes roaring out of Grand Coulee Dam. But that surge of energy is channeled into transformers that make it adaptable for human usage. In some like fashion, the inscrutable Almighty has transformed Himself into the likeness of a man so that we can relate to Him without being blown away.

Sense the unimaginable wonder of this transformation in a poem by Russell Ogden:

Is this God---This tiny babe in its cradle rude
With bands of severed cloth entwined, With oxen stalled?
These peasant folk of lowly mien,
These herdsmen, rough, unkempt,
Is this God—This tiny babe in its cradle rude
This filthy straw, the stench, the grime—Can this be God?
Is this a King—This untaught Galilean doctrining His
motley band?
What purpose the vile throng hailing a bibber of wine,
fellow of sinners,
Transient prophet, wanting of wealth and home–can this be
a King?
Is this a man—this wretched form with visage marred,
Congealed in spittle and in blood,
Of garments reft? Protracted joints and riven flesh the shape
deform.
The frenzied mob a fiendish beast have surely killed—Can it
be a man?
From sacred lore a lightning smites upon my soul,
As prophets call thy name above all names:
Immanuel, and David's Son, and Paschal Lamb—
My Savior and my God!

Jesus Christ continues to be either the rock of stumbling or the chief cornerstone of life. We must either worship Him as Almighty God historically revealed in human flesh or revile Him as a liar or lunatic. There is no middle ground.

Jesus is neither liar nor lunatic. The historical record gives no credence to either claim. Astounding as it may seem, He is exactly whom He claimed to be, the Messiah, the Son of God in human flesh. Because of who He is, we must give careful attention to what He says in this final Passover dialogue with His disciples. In a legitimate sense we can label His words as a "deathbed" statement.

114

He spoke only hours away from His agonizing death on the cross. Any of the issues He introduced were close to His heart.

God has laid on my heart the issue He prayed earnestly about just before He and His disciples exited the Passover celebration. Let me quote once more His closing plea to His Father. Notice the intensity of His petition: *"My prayer is not for them alone. I pray also for those who will believe in Me through their message, that all of them may be ONE, Father, just as You are in Me and I am in You. May they also be in Us so that the world may believe that You have sent Me. I have given them the glory that You gave Me, that they may be ONE as We are One: I in them and You in Me. May they be brought to complete UNITY to let the world know that You sent Me and have loved them even as You have loved Me."* (John 17:20-23)

You will notice that Jesus included you and me in His prayer: *"I pray also for those who will believe in Me through their message, that all of them may be ONE, Father."* The amazing thing is not just that He prayed that we all may be bound together in unity but for a oneness that mirrors the unity within the Trinity of Father, Son and Holy Spirit. In John 16 Jesus speaks of the ministry of the Holy Spirit Whom He will send to indwell His disciples. He no doubt astounds the disciples when He says, *"It is for your good that I am going away. Unless I go away the Counselor will not come to you: but if I go, I will send Him to you."* (vs. 7) It is the indwelling Holy Spirit Who brings the believer into intimate fellowship with other believers, *"That all of them may be one."* (vs. 21) It is the same Holy Spirit who unites us with the Father and the Son, thus reflecting the unity within the Trinity, *"That they may be one as We are one."* (vs. 22) It is not that we have the unique unity that binds the Father, Son and Holy Spirit into one divine Being. That is reserved for the eternal, transcendent God. But it is a unity orchestrated by the Holy Spirit that enables us to break out of our self-centered nature and reflect God's self-giving love. *"Be completely humble and gentle; be patient, bearing with one another in love. Make every effort to keep the unity of the Spirit through the bond of peace."* (Ephesians 4:2-3)

Since the indwelling Holy Spirit is the divine Agent producing unity, I was faced with a dilemma concerning the traditional

115

Pentecostal doctrine of Spirit baptism. My Pentecostal church tradition taught that all valid Spirit baptisms must be accompanied by speaking in tongues. There is no scriptural support for this tradition and many Christians, including many Charismatic groups, reject it. This doctrine creates major division within the body of Christ. This makes the Holy Spirit the author of division if the Pentecostal tradition is true. My dilemma is this: Do I trust the Holy Spirit to promote the unity Jesus prayed for or do I trust my Pentecostal tradition that produces disunity? I chose to distrust my tradition. I knew the Holy Spirit would never be responsible for hindering the Father from answering the Son's request for unity.

I must reiterate, the issue is not about speaking in tongues. The issue is the erroneous and divisive purpose which we Pentecostals assigned to tongues. I am so grateful for the gift of tongues which has blessed my life for many years. I am saddened that the purpose of this sign gift has been demoted. It has been lowered to a level that produces disunity among Christians. Tongues have a far loftier purpose. We Pentecostals need to elevate them to the honorable place given them in Scripture.

Some may wonder why I make such a big deal of opposing the Pentecostal tradition which makes tongues a necessary sign of Spirit baptism. Let me briefly answer:

(1) The spiritual unity of the church is a critical issue to Jesus Christ, as is clear from His prayer in John 17. I make a big deal out of opposing the Pentecostal tradition because unity is "a big deal" to Jesus and should be to His followers.

(2) I believe the Father is going to answer Jesus' prayer for unity before His Son returns to establish His eternal kingdom. The sooner unity prevails, the sooner our Lord will come again. Peter exhorts God's people to do what can be done to "speed its coming."

(3) The truth of Scripture must always take priority over tradition.

The Pentecostal tradition is built on a series of assumptions without solid support of Scripture. As Joel clearly points out, Pentecostal tongues were given as a sign affirming that all language groups, all nations, all races and skin colors (all humanity, all flesh) were now eligible to be filled with the Spirit. Individuals from all people groups could now be saved without first converting to Judaism. The Old Covenant was no longer in effect. The New Covenant was ushered in with the symbol of tongues to mark the transition to the universality of the gospel. The "tongues" of ancient Babel brought division to a world in rebellion against God. The tongues of Pentecost were God's sign of unity in Christ that transcends language distinctions. How could I not protest against the divisive distortion of the purpose of tongues that became the distinctive of my church?

CHAPTER 9

A THEOLOGY BASED ON EXPERIENCE RATHER THAN REVEALED TRUTH

I have found it extremely difficult to get traditional Pentecostals to engage in an honest search of Scripture regarding the purpose of tongues that accompanied Spirit baptism at Pentecost and subsequently. The one passage always quoted is Acts 2:4: "All of them were filled with the Holy Spirit and began to speak in other tongues as the Spirit enabled them." This is the historical record of WHAT happened (tongues) but it leaves us clueless as to WHY it happened. Joel's prophecy (Acts 2:17-21) provides the WHY, (tongues symbolize all language groups) giving the reason for the WHAT. Isaiah enabled Paul to see the WHO (unbelievers) the WHAT was for. Luke the historian gives the WHERE (Jerusalem) and WHEN (Pentecost feast) tongues first accompanied Spirit baptism. This set the pattern for subsequent outpourings on other people groups. The WHY of tongues is explained by Joel and applies to the outpouring on Roman Gentiles (Acts 10:45-6) and Asian Gentiles in Ephesus (Acts 19:7).

When I ask a Pentecostal friend why he insists that his tradition is absolutely true, the answer is not based on Scripture. His conviction is based on personal experience. Experience is important and I treasure supernatural experiences by which the Holy Spirit has enriched my life. How barren the Christian life would be without those awesome times when the Holy Spirit lifts us into the heavenly realm of God's manifested presence. But for spiritual experiences, divorced from rock-solid biblical support, to serve as a foundation for religious truth is a formula for confusion and delusion.

To base a doctrine on experience with no Scripture to confirm it is a passport to error, if not heresy. We see this illustrated in the early history of Pentecostalism. When the Assemblies of God was being organized, there was great conflict between the Trinitarians and those who were popularly known as "Jesus Only" or "Oneness" people. The latter believed that Jesus was the one and only divine person who revealed Himself in three different modes or roles as Father, Son and Holy Spirit. Several who were prominent in the formation of the Assemblies of God switched their allegiance to "Jesus Only." The historical record of Pentecostalism clearly reveals that the reason for the switch was because "Jesus Only" adherents seemed to have more frequent and more spectacular spiritual experiences. These experiences "proved" their doctrine was truly from God despite Scripture to the contrary.

Modalism is the theological term usually used for belief in "Jesus Only". This was a heresy that the early church faced and dealt with in the third century. The chief proponent of this position today is The United Pentecostal Church. What is true now concerning the modalistic United Pentecostal Church was true at its formation a hundred years ago. Adherents declared vehemently that their teaching must be true. "Look at how people baptized in Jesus' name only come out of the water speaking in tongues and prophesying. God is attesting to the truth of our doctrine." Using experience as the ultimate test for truth about the formula for water baptism and the essence of God, rather than the revelation in Scripture, appealed to many Pentecostals a hundred years ago. Even E. N. Bell, the first General Superintendent of the Assemblies of God, was so swayed by the experiential test for truth he succumbed to being rebaptized in Jesus' name. To his credit, he later reversed his acceptance of Modalism (Jesus Only) and affirmed his belief in the Trinity. (Ibid. Blumhofer, p. 225)

Because Pentecostalism was so enamored with religious experiences, personal experience trumped Scripture as the measure of truth. It was especially true for Oneness adherents but carried over into the Assemblies of God. Howard Goss, one of the early leaders of the Assemblies of God, "acknowledged the pressure among Pentecostal preachers to present 'new light' and 'fresh insights.'" Blumhofer goes on to say, "While responsible Pentecostals maintained that 'new teaching' had to demonstrate continuity with Scripture, they often seemed torn between two sources of authority: the objective Word and the subjective Spirit. Otherwise, they forced Scripture to accommodate their revelations. In the end, however, some Pentecostals opted (though most would not admit it) for the Spirit as the final source of authority. Howard Goss (who became a prominent Oneness leader) reportedly admitted: 'You'll never get this studying it out like some other doctrine. This comes by revelation." (Ibid. p. 229 The Assemblies of God leadership followed Scripture in regards to the Trinity but they succumbed to subjective experience when formulating the purpose of tongues.

As the 1918 General Council drew closer, it was announced that "all the major doctrines of the Assemblies of God would be discussed." I found no record of this taking place. Apparently the key decision makers had become committed to "evidential tongues." *The Christian Evangel,* official periodical for the Assemblies, ran a series of articles favoring the evidential purpose of tongues. Fred Bosworth, a strong proponent of the primacy of Scripture, wrote a powerful scriptural argument against what had become known as the "classical" Pentecostal position on tongues. The *Evangel* editor refused to publish it. Another leader opposing Bosworth had spread a malicious, untrue story that produced a split in his Dallas congregation. Others declared he had no right to retain his credentials. Rather than continue to fight for a scriptural solution to the issue of the purpose of tongues, Bosworth surrendered to the primacy of experience over Scripture. As I point out elsewhere, Bosworth didn't dispute that tongues were a gift of the Spirit. He affirmed the gift but denied Scripture lent any evidential purpose to this gift for Spirit baptism.

Since this doctrine does not have a solid biblical foundation, what makes it so difficult to alter? As suggested earlier, doctrines can be changed between disputants if there is a mutually agreed authority which can be appealed to. For us evangelicals, that authority is the Bible.

Pentecostals appeal to Scripture but it clearly does not prove their position. The Bible is not the glue that keeps the doctrine intact. Rather, the doctrine has transmuted into a tradition hallowed by stories, experiences, and hero figures. Tragically, these have had more holding power than the Bible.

Tradition made it difficult, almost impossible, for Jesus to connect with the Pharisees. It is tradition that also prevents the cessationists from acknowledging that the gifts of the Spirit are supernaturally manifested in the church today. Yet I am convinced that there are multitudes (the vast majority, in fact) within the Assemblies of God, and multitudes of cessationists, who hold to

Scripture as the inspired Word of God. Eventually, the truth of Scripture will overcome tradition. It must.

Right now the body of Christ is fractured. Our Assemblies of God position, if we really wholeheartedly believe it, logically forces us to say that everyone who has not spoken in tongues has not been filled with the Holy Spirit. That simply isn't true. Jesus must be terribly grieved that this doctrine, based upon assumptions, erroneous conclusions, mislabeled experiences and fallacious reasoning, splinters His body, the church.

FOUNDATIONS BUILT BY A RACIST INSTIGATOR

In the early days of the Pentecostal outpouring, the position that tongues must be the initial physical evidence of the baptism in the Holy Spirit was questioned by many godly people, for good reason. Charles Parham, the chief instigator of this position, was of questionable character. Edith Blumhofer, an Assemblies of God historian, points out his strong racist tendencies. (Edith Blumhofer, *The Assemblies of God, Vol. I,* p. 108-9) It is significant that one of the purposes for the "sign" of tongues was to break down racial prejudices. No wonder Parham overlooked that and proclaimed something more esoteric and dramatic. He was unorthodox in many of his beliefs.

Blumhofer further states: *"Parham's doctrinal inventiveness led to his advocating a variety of unusual interpretations of Scripture to meet such age-old questions as 'Where did Cain get his wife?' For example, he distinguished between 'created' and 'formed' humanity, claiming that all created humanity perished in the flood, whereas, through Noah, Adam's line of 'formed' humanity was preserved. Thus, Cain's wife was created, whereas Cain was formed."* (Ibid. p. 75)

Blumhofer describes other idiosyncrasies. Parham was convinced that tongues were given to enable missionaries to proclaim the gospel without having to study the foreign language of those they ministered to. Many zealous people with the gift of tongues went to foreign lands fully believing they would be able to communicate to the natives by speaking in tongues. They had not been grounded in Scripture or they would have seen the folly of this. Many became disillusioned while others got stranded in far-off foreign countries, and other orthodox missionaries had to rescue them and support them until they could return home. It did not lead to an outpouring of goodwill.

Shortly after the Azusa Street revival, respected evangelical leaders began to be concerned about excesses. One such leader was A. B. Simpson, founder of the Christian and Missionary Alliance Church. Simpson was not opposed to tongues but he was opposed to declaring them the initial physical evidence of being baptized in the Spirit. He could find no scriptural support for this and he kindly, but publicly, cautioned believers about accepting this doctrine. A number of Alliance members were filled with the Spirit and Alliance leaders diligently attempted to differentiate between the genuine and the spurious.

"The conviction that Pentecostals misread the Bible—that the Bible, although affirming the presence of tongues speech in the early church, neither advocated any uniform initial evidence of Spirit baptism nor distinguished between evidential tongues, the gift of tongues, and the use of tongues in private worship—was central to the crystallizing of an Alliance position on Pentecostalism. . . .

"On April 13, 1914, the Alliance articulated its official position: We believe that the gift of tongues or speaking in tongues did in many cases in the apostolic church accompany or follow the baptism of the Holy Spirit. We believe also that other supernatural and even miraculous operations on the part of the Holy Spirit through His people are competent and possible according to the sovereign will of the Holy Spirit Himself throughout the Christian age. But we hold that none of these manifestations are essentially connected with the baptism of the Holy Spirit, and that the consecrated believer may receive the Spirit in His fullness without speaking in tongues or any miraculous manifestations whatever; and that no Christian teacher has the right to require such manifestations as evidence of the baptism of the Holy Spirit. The teachings of the Apostle Paul in First Corinthians, chapters 12-14, make this exceedingly plain." (Ibid. p. 295)

The stance of the Alliance was brotherly and opened the door to scriptural investigation. The Alliance leaders decided to treat tongues-speaking as they did several other controversial issues. *"It would be wise,"* they said, *"to leave the question of 'the Latter*

Rain' and related doctrines, as matters of personal liberty, just as the question of baptism, church government, and other differences of belief among the evangelical bodies. "

Several Pentecostal leaders were strongly influenced by the Alliance position. Although the sane and scriptural Alliance position was rejected by Pentecostals, this view has made a powerful comeback among millions of Pentecostals and Charismatics who do not insist that tongues must validate Spirit baptisms. Professor Allen Anderson's research supports this. *"Many Pentecostal groups, including some of the largest Pentecostal churches in Europe and Latin America and many of the so-called Charismatic Movement, do not insist on the 'initial evidence' of tongues."* Tongues do accompany many Spirit baptisms but the purpose, as Joel indicates, is to symbolize all the languages of mankind to which the gospel must be proclaimed. This unifying purpose was true at Pentecost and is true today.

Speaking in tongues accompanied my Spirit baptism and I assumed that it was evidence of valid baptism. However, this conclusion was based on what I had been indoctrinated to accept as the necessary evidence. It was years later that I discovered the lack of Scripture to undergird this teaching. Even more years passed before I understood the meaning of tongues strongly supported by Scripture. Tragically, what God designed to promote Christian unity among people of every language became a sign of spiritual elitism that promoted a nonnegotiable dogma.

The dramatic experience of speaking in tongues hijacked the Pentecostal experience of empowerment by the Holy Spirit. By that I mean Spirit baptism is essentially an experience in which the Holy Spirit anoints believers with supernatural power for combating the satanic forces of evil. Multitudes of Pentecostals have settled for speaking in tongues instead of the power which Jesus promised. Of course, many traditional Pentecostals have received both tongues and empowerment and we rejoice in that. We do not rejoice in their divisive insistence that one has never been Spirit baptized unless validated by tongues. Religious experience must never supersede the Word of God as the test of truth. Matthew 7:22-23 supplies a vivid example of this principle: *"Many will say to Me on that day, 'Lord, Lord, did we not prophesy in Your name, and in Your name drive out demons and perform many miracles?' Then I will tell them plainly, 'I never knew you.Away from Me, you evildoers!' "*

After *Pentecost Revisited* was published, I traveled extensively talking to other Pentecostal preachers about issues raised in my book. Many agree with my scriptural exegesis but they were unwilling to risk taking a stand against the imbedded tradition. It might cost them their church or their position within the denomination. Loyalty to denominational tradition triumphed over scriptural truth. Why rock the boat?

Friends have scolded me with brotherly concern: "Glenn, your teaching about unity in the body of Christ will be undermined by creating disunity within the Assemblies of God." My aim is not to create disunity within the church I served in for more than half a century. Disunity already exists. Many give lip service to our tradition but hesitate to proclaim it because they struggle with the lack of solid biblical support. Churches even change their names so as not to be identified as Assemblies of God or Pentecostal. This, despite the denomination's attempt to get every member church to publicly display its affiliation. Unity within a denomination whose distinctive, nonnegotiable tradition promotes spiritual elitism will inevitably foster divisiveness within the Body of Christ. Eventually, disunity will erupt within the denomination itself. It may take decades or even centuries before biblical truth replaces imbedded divisive tradition. The Holy Spirit will never cease working in the hearts of Christians to bring about the fulfillment of Christ's prayer: *"That they may be one as We are one: I in them and You in Me. May they be brought to complete unity to let the world know that You have sent Me and have loved them even as You have loved Me."* (John 17:22-23)

Another lament from a close friend steeped in traditional Pentecostalism needs to be faced. He fears my position will discourage people from seeking to be baptized in the Holy Spirit. This is an irrational fear, perhaps aroused by another fear, the risk of losing denominational control over what determines Spirit baptism. Jesus is the sovereign Baptizer in the Holy Spirit. Once He is released from the traditional box in which we have tried to imprison Him, I have reason to believe many more people will become candidates for Spirit baptism.

I have seen a remarkable openness to the supernatural ministry of the Holy Spirit by those who have read *Pentecost Revisited.* Cessationists see the futility of their position and many are thirsty for the anointing and power of the Holy Spirit. As world conditions deteriorate and the forces of evil become increasingly pronounced, more and more of God's people will cry out for a mighty endowment of spiritual power.

Professor Charles Kraft of Fuller Seminary and former missionary to Nigeria has cautioned: *"We can no longer afford to send missionaries and national church leaders back to their fields or to send young people to the missions field for the first time without teaching them how to heal the sick and cast out demons."* (Quoted by Prof. Peter Wagner in *Perspectives*, 4th Edition, p. 582)

As more and more missionaries discover that they can partake of the mighty power of the Holy Spirit without speaking in tongues, we will see the supernatural power of God increasingly displayed. This would have happened long ago were it not for Pentecostal extremists.

Naturally, questions have arisen because of what I have written. Some of my best insights have resulted from questions I have had to wrestle with. Questions are healthy and helpful if they motivate one to search for truth. Here is a question you may have asked, as I certainly have: "If tongues are not the absolutely required initial evidence of Spirit baptism, why has there been so much numerical growth among Pentecostals who teach this?" I suggest you consider the following:

First, the Holy Spirit will bless the proclamation of the gospel by whomever it is preached. Paul rejoiced that the gospel was proclaimed, even by his adversaries. Although many Pentecostals misunderstood the purpose of tongues that accompanied Spirit baptism, they nevertheless received the outpouring of the Spirit. It is the presence and power of the Holy Spirit, not tongues, that produces an effective witness that leads to growth in the body of Christ.

Second, misidentifying the purpose of tongues did not nullify the purpose of Spirit baptism. *"But you will receive power when the Holy Spirit comes on you; and you will be my witnesses in Jerusalem, and in all Judea and Samaria, and to the ends of the earth."* (Acts 1:8) The Joel passage quoted by Peter (Acts 2:17-21) affirms that the purpose of tongues that accompany Spirit baptism is to signify that all languages, races and people groups are equally welcome into Christ's kingdom, ("*EVERYONE who calls on the name of the Lord will be saved.*" *[Acts 2:21]),* thus promoting the unity Christ desired for His people. It should not be surprising that Spirit baptism accomplished what the Spirit ordained be done, i.e., anoint believers to proclaim the gospel with power to "the ends of the earth." I firmly believe that if tongues that accompanied Spirit baptisms following the outpouring at Azusa Street had been recognized for what they truly were, the symbol of all language groups on earth, even greater growth would have resulted. We would have avoided white Pentecostals practicing apartheid in South Africa and flagrant racism in the United States. Furthermore, abuses, misuses, counterfeit manifestations and all the disunity and divisiveness associated with making tongues the required initial evidence of Spirit baptism would have been largely avoided.

Not all Pentecostals involved in rapid growth of the Church require evidential tongues as proof of Spirit baptism. Millions of Pentecostal believers do not speak in tongues. Let me remind you again of the words of Pentecostal scholar, Dr. Allan Anderson of Birmingham University (England): "Many Pentecostal groups, including some of the largest Pentecostal churches in Europe and Latin America and many in the so-called Charismatic Movement, do not insist on the 'initial evidence' of tongues. . . . It may be very difficult to tell what is meant by 'Pentecostal' today, but perhaps the term is best understood as referring to those movements with an emphasis on the experience of the power of the Holy Spirit with accompanying manifestations of the imminent presence of God." (Dr. A. Anderson, "The Origins, Growth and Significance of the Pentecostal Movements of the Third World") I say a hearty "Amen" to that characterization. It fits the New Testament record and places the emphasis squarely where it should be.

The "Jesus Only" branch of Pentecostalism has also seen remarkable growth, boasting more than four-million global adherents. Does that confirm the truth of its doctrine?

When the experience of being baptized in the Holy Spirit is no longer irrevocably tied to the physical evidence of tongues which can be counterfeited, abused and misused, then sincere believers will trust Christ to baptize them as He chooses.

Fred F. Bosworth, a pioneer Pentecostal a century ago, warned that Scripture and reason should never be usurped by experiences and assumptions. Here is something he wrote that is worthy of careful thought: *"The word 'evidence' in the Scriptures is never used in connection with a spiritual gift or manifestation, making faith to depend upon any sign or physical manifestation, but the Apostle distinctly states that 'faith is the evidence.' Anything that is to be received in answer to prayer is to be received by faith, even the great miracle of the new birth, and Paul expressly states that we are to 'receive the promise of the Spirit through faith.'"* (Galatians 3:14)

When I was initially filled with the Holy Spirit, what impressed and encouraged me was that Jesus had kept His promise. I actually had power to overcome temptations and resist evil, which I had never had before. Because of the Pentecostal tradition in which I had been reared, I think the Lord may have provided the gift of tongues to accompany my baptism just to reassure me. But to me, the increased spiritual power, not tongues, was the evidence of a valid Spirit baptism. When Jesus baptizes a believer in the Spirit, I believe the recipient will know it has happened. There may not be a highly charged emotional response, or there may be. Jesus, the Baptizer, is the sovereign Lord of this baptismal event. We freely and joyfully acknowledge His sovereignty and surrender to His Lordship. Some may speak in tongues, some may not. But all will experience a fresh power and anointing for service and "character construction".

God deals with each of us individually. He knows us, He loves us, and He has a plan for each unique life. He wants to baptize you in the Holy Spirit to empower you, to gift you, and to enable you to eventually become like Jesus Christ. He will decide the manifestation(s) of the Spirit appropriate for you and your situation. He may flood your soul with such overwhelming love that you want to embrace the whole world. Or He may electrify you with overflowing joy that fills your heart with glorious song. Or He may lead you to speak out in a language He provides. Or you may experience all of these or something else that He tailors just for you.

"Tailor" is a fitting word. Jesus tells His disciple just before His ascension, "I am going to send you what my Father has promised: but stay in the city until you have been clothed with power from on high." (Luke 24:49) Jesus is the master "Tailor" who clothes us with the Holy Spirit. He does not provide a "one size fits all" garment. He takes into consideration all our "measurements" . . . our personalities, our strengths, our weaknesses, our culture, our genetic and environmental backgrounds. We can't all wear identical clothes, nor does Jesus baptize everyone in the Holy Spirit in the same fashion. But you can be assured of this: He has a purpose and plan for your life that takes everything into consideration. He will see to it that you are spiritually attired properly for every occasion when you invite Him to clothe you with power from on high. Jesus, who loves you and died for you, is the Baptizer.

You can trust Him. The experience of being baptized in the Holy Spirit will be a wonderful, transforming encounter between you and Jesus as He empowers you with the same Spirit that empowered Him.

I believe adopting Anderson's criteria rather than insisting that tongues is the absolute required evidence of Spirit baptism would produce a fresh outpouring of "manifestations of the imminent presence of God." There is an increasing hunger for genuine supernatural manifestations of the Holy Spirit. Frankly, many Christians have seen so much sham, commercialism and fraud associated with elements in Pentecostalism that they have become suspicious about claims of miracles and supernatural manifestations of the Holy Spirit. At least, this is true in the Western world. I believe our tradition has contributed to this sad, sad state of affairs. I am willing to risk suffering, if need be, for the sake of defending truth. There is a sense in which I may even find joy in doing so. I cannot find joy in defending or supporting a questionable and divisive religious tradition.

Let me reflect back forty-plus years. At that time I had no insight as to the purpose of tongues that accompanied Spirit baptism. However, I knew there was no scriptural foundation for insisting that Jesus Christ (the Baptizer) must authenticate every one He baptized in the Spirit with tongues. The only criteria He must meet were those He had imposed on Himself. Jesus Himself had declared that the baptism in the Holy Spirit would provide an impartation of spiritual power which will enable His followers to bear witness to Jesus as Lord to all people everywhere (Acts 1:8).

Listen carefully to the Chief Shepherd and meditate upon the simplicity of His pronouncement: "You will receive power when the Holy Spirit comes on you; and you will be My witnesses . . ." (Acts 1:8) That's not very spectacular or dramatic, is it? But if believed, proclaimed, and acted upon, it will absolutely transform the character of the church.

DEVELOPING THE CHARACTER DISPLAYED BY JESUS

The sign or evidence that the Holy Spirit has come upon a believer is power that produces people who exhibit Christ-like character. "Witnesses" is a plural noun, not a verb. Jesus is not referring to what we say about Him. He is declaring that the proof of being baptized (immersed) in the Holy Spirit is demonstrating a character like the Holy Spirit produced in Jesus.

Jesus was truly man. He laid aside His divine prerogatives, and all He was and did was accomplished in the power of the Holy Spirit. Luke records that when our Lord began His ministry, "Jesus, full of the Holy Spirit, returned from the Jordan and was led by the Spirit into the desert." (Luke 4:1) Even more definitively, Peter proclaims in his sermon to Cornelius' household:

"You know what has happened throughout Judea, beginning in Galilee after the baptism that John preached—how God anointed Jesus of Nazareth with the Holy Spirit and power, and how He went around doing good and healing all who were under the power of the devil, because God was with Him." (Acts 10:38)

The same Holy Spirit that anointed and empowered Jesus has been dispatched to anoint and empower all His followers. This power provides tremendous potential but it has to be channeled into development of Christ-like character and Christ-like service. And what are the character qualities of Jesus that we are to emulate so as to bear witness to Him? Paul describes them: *"The fruit of the Spirit is love, joy, peace, patience, kindness, goodness, faithfulness, gentleness, and self-control.... Since we live by the Spirit, let us keep in step with the Spirit. Let us not become conceited, provoking and envying each other."* (Galatians 5:22, 25-26)

EXERCISING SPIRITUAL GIFTS

A further proof of being Spirit-filled is the manifestation of spiritual gifts. Paul affirms this very positively:

"Now to each one the manifestation of the Spirit is given for the common good. To one there is given through the Spirit the ability to speak with wisdom, to another the ability to speak with knowledge by means of the same Spirit, to another faith by the same Spirit, to another gifts of healing by that one Spirit, to another miraculous powers, to another prophecy, to another the ability to distinguish between spirits, to another the ability to speak in different kinds of tongues. All these are the work of one and the same Spirit, and He gives them to each man, just as He determines." (1 Corinthians 12:7-11)

Paul doesn't say, "Now to each apostle...." This passage has universal application to all believers. Also, there is no time limitation; it is as applicable today as when Paul wrote it.

The gifts of the Spirit Paul enumerated to the Corinthians were not meant to be the totality. In Romans Paul provides more of the divine gifts the Spirit brings to believers to advance and build up the church.

"Just as each one of us has one body with many members, and these members do not all have the same function, so in Christ we who are many form one body, and each member belongs to all others. We have different gifts, according to the grace given us. If a man's gift is prophesying, let him use it in proportion to his faith. If it is serving, let him serve; if it is teaching, let him teach; if it is encouraging, let him encourage; if it is contributing to the needs of others, let him give generously; if it is leadership, let him govern diligently; if it is showing mercy, let him do it cheerfully." (Romans 12:4-8)

RESULTS OF WRONGFUL INTERPRETATION OF THE PURPOSE OF TONGUES

If the fruit and gifts of the Spirit had been identified as the evidence of being filled with the Spirit, think what a profound difference it would have made in the church. Consider, first of all, what evils would have been reduced or even eliminated.

• Counterfeit tongues, prophecies, and miracles would have lost their appeal.

These have abounded and still do. My mother used to tell me, "Son, the devil can counterfeit everything God does except a holy life." The fruit and gifts of the Spirit work together to build up the church and bring glory to her Lord. Only one gift is designed to edify the individual and that is the gift of tongues when it is exercised in accordance with Scripture. It is not a gift for public ministry but for personal, private communication with God (1 Corinthians 14:2, 4). I delight in praying, and sometimes singing, in the Spirit. But I do it in my "prayer closet" and no one is invited in, not even my wife. When we pray together, it is in English. There is no prohibition against our praying together in tongues. That's just my personal idiosyncrasy.

• Rampant disunity would have been avoided within Christianity in general, as well as within Pentecostalism in particular.

The schism between cessationists and Pentecostals could have been more easily breached. If the church had seen the true and intended fruit of the Holy Spirit build up the whole body of Christ, a hunger for the fullness of the Spirit would have grown. Not only did the invalid evidence of tongues produce division with the entire body of Christ, but it spawned division within Pentecostalism. Dr. Allan Anderson laments, "The Pentecostal movement split in less than a century into 'nearly as many different divisions as it took the rest of the church a millennium to produce', and as a result has not lived up to its ecumenical potential." (Dr. Allan Anderson, An Introduction to Pentecostalism, p. 250) The manifestation designed to break down barriers instead produced more.

• Many years of racial strife and injustice could well have been avoided if the church had allowed the Spirit to do in Los Angeles what He had done in Caesarea and Samaria two millennia before.

The Holy Spirit's falling upon the black church was God's signal that members of this people group were full-fledged members of His family. The signal was to the unbelieving white church; however, they rejected His sign and substituted their own, making tongues a required evidence of valid Spirit baptism. For the better part of another century, eleven o'clock on Sunday morning continued to be the most segregated hour in America. Pastor Seymour was baptized in the Holy Spirit and spoke in tongues, but he rejected the dogma that tongues were the sign of his infilling. Did he sense there was something wrong with a tradition that forced him to sit out in the hall all alone rather than in Parham's classroom with his white classmates?

• Spiritual caste systems would not have arisen. There are no second-class citizens in God's kingdom, whether based on race or spiritual experiences. The apostle Paul endured a "thorn" in his flesh for many years. The thorn was a painful reminder from God to keep him from boasting about his spiritual experiences (2 Corinthians 12:7).

WHAT COULD THE CHURCH HAVE GAINED IF WE'D ACCEPTED OUR LORD'S WORDS?

• Our impact upon the culture would have been profound. The supernatural power of the Holy Spirit demonstrated through individuals graced by love, joy, peace and the other character traits of our Lord would have advanced the cause of Christ and His kingdom immensely.

• The gifts of the Spirit would have abounded more profusely and more powerfully, freed from the limitations that improper use of tongues imposed.

It was not immediately apparent to me that only half of Jesus' criteria concerning the outpouring of the Holy Spirit was fulfilled at Pentecost. All the waiting disciples received an impartation of spiritual power. What I initially failed to see is that Pentecost did not equip the disciples to be witnesses "to the ends of the earth."

All followers of Jesus at Pentecost were still in bondage to their ancient Jewish tradition. They did not believe Gentiles could be part of the Christian community without submitting to Mosaic rites demanded of proselytes. Jesus never fulfilled the promise of Acts 1:8 until eight years later when the Holy Spirit was poured out on the Roman army garrison in Caesarea. The Spirit baptism of the assembled Gentiles was accompanied by tongues, to the consternation and utter amazement of Peter and his Jewish companions. It was Caesarea that opened the door for the gospel to go to the ends of the earth. Tongues at Caesarea signified to Peter that his prejudiced view of the gospel would no longer be countenanced by Jesus. Thus we see that one of the chief purposes of tongues accompanying Spirit baptism was to be an ongoing reminder that the gospel was for all people groups, all races, all languages and cultures.

The outpouring of the Holy Spirit at Los Angeles' Azusa Street in 1906 is a significant historical occasion. A largely black congregation led by a pastor whose parents had been slaves suddenly became the focus of the religious world. Blacks and whites, ministers and laymen and curious onlookers of all colors and backgrounds gathered to see what was going on. Los Angeles now joined Jerusalem, Caesarea and Ephesus as a site where the Holy Spirit had been outpoured accompanied by speaking in tongues. The secular press had a field day ridiculing the strange phenomena that accompanied this Divine visitation. It was essentially the same response Luke describes when scoffers heard the one hundred disciples speaking tongues en masse in Jerusalem: "These people are drunk."

We should not be surprised that the secular world misunderstood what was taking place at Azusa Street. The press played up the spectacular because it sold papers. But they had absolutely no insight about supernatural manifestations of the Holy Spirit. A far greater tragedy is that the Christian world misunderstood what God was doing at Azusa Street. In a fashion nearly as dramatic as the outpouring on the Gentiles at Caesarea, God poured out His Spirit upon black Americans. They were a people only a generation out of slavery, still economically deprived, forced to accept second-class citizenship and endure the humiliation which accompanied their status.

Azusa Street was God's sign to unbelievers. No, not to unbelievers in the pagan, secular world. It was a sign to unbelieving white Christians in America and around the world. What did they not believe? They did not believe that black human beings were fully equal to whites. They did not believe blacks should be fully integrated into American society and into the family of God. We white Christians were as bound by tradition and prejudice against blacks as Simon Peter and the early Jewish Christians were against Gentiles. I am not pointing fingers. If I had been present then I likely would have done the same, although it pains me to acknowledge this.

Jesus used the same supernatural sign at Azusa Street as He had at Caesarea to break the wall of partition between people groups. The sign was an unexpected and mighty outpouring of the Holy Spirit accompanied by tongues upon a largely black congregation. Christians in many places had been praying for God to pour out His Spirit again as He had on the apostolic Church. Many of these spiritually thirsty people flocked to Los Angeles to see what was happening. Those with hungry and receptive hearts were filled with the Spirit and spoke in tongues.

There was a wonderful spirit of love and acceptance among the diverse racial groups that gathered. For a short time God's people seemed to understand the sign of tongues. Was Jesus' prayer for unity among His followers at last to be answered? Unfortunately, the positive response to the sign of tongues was short lived. Before three years had passed a divisive spirit shattered the love and harmony that initially prevailed. The sign not only was rejected, it was so altered it became unrecognizable. The tongues of Azusa were Christ's sign that blacks were to be accepted into the Christian community without prejudice. The sign was not received. The scourge of racism continued, nurtured and encouraged by Charles Parham. He was the talented Pentecostal preacher who first insisted that tongues must accompany Spirit baptism or it was invalid.

The sign designated to bring various people groups together in unity was transformed into a sign that fostered division. How did this happen? It happened largely because the purpose of tongues at Pentecost was overlooked by all but a few discerning students of Scripture. The fascination with the spectacular was more alluring than serious exegetical study of pertinent Scripture. Also, the American culture was predominantly racist. A symbol that pointed to racial and ethnic equality would have been as hard for white America to accept as it was for the Jewish Christians at Pentecost. Because of this inability, further decades of racial strife resulted. God had to use the power of civil government to enforce changes that the body of Christ should have voluntarily initiated and promoted.

For forty years I shared my conviction that speaking in tongues was not the initial physical evidence of Spirit baptism with denominational officials via the annual credential renewal form required of Assemblies of God ministers. Joe Gerhart, the Northern California and Nevada District Superintendent, was aware of my stance when he invited me to transfer to his District in 1969. Leaders in this District continued for the next four decades to recommend to national headquarters that my credentials be renewed. I will always be grateful to them for trusting my integrity and extending their friendship. As long as I was ministering in an Assemblies of God church, I never revealed my disagreement with the Pentecostal tradition on evidential tongues.

I knew what was wrong with the traditional interpretation concerning the purpose of tongues that accompanied Spirit baptism. It was a tradition built on a series of invalid assumptions. But tongues did occur so there must have been a divine purpose. I sought the Lord for insight into this conundrum and He graciously opened my eyes to the Old Testament prophecies of Isaiah and Joel as quoted by the apostles Paul and Peter. At last, all the pertinent Old Testament and New Testament Scriptures fit together harmoniously. Tongues were God's sign that the divisive tongues of Babel could be reversed. How can this reversal occur? It can happen when God's people recognize that the tongues of Pentecost symbolized all the language groups, all the races, all the cultures of the world. It will happen when God's people recognize the significance of Joel's prophetic announcement. "God says, The Holy Spirit will be outpoured on all humanity. . . . Everyone who calls on the Lord will be saved." It can happen when Pentecostals adopt a scriptural understanding of the tongues of Pentecost.

When I finally understood the scriptural purpose for tongues, it was a gloriously freeing experience for me. I now enjoy defending speaking in tongues. When I show from Scripture that tongues are God's sign that all language groups, races and nationalities are equally precious to God and equally welcome to be part of His kingdom, their faces light up. Dialogue does not deteriorate into heated argumentation. I have seen a new openness to the supernatural manifestations of the Holy Spirit.

Once we Pentecostals get our doctrine concerning the purpose of tongues on a solid biblical foundation, many of the abuses that embarrass us will disappear. We will no longer have to cringe when someone begins to relate an embarrassingly unscriptural incident they observed at a Pentecostal service. That will be a great day for biblical Pentecostalism and a great day for advancing God's kingdom with genuine "signs" following.

Thank God, multitudes of Pentecostals/Charismatics do not adhere to the divisive position on tongues as "initial evidence," as Allan Anderson has pointed out. We Pentecostals boast of having five-hundred million adherents spread across the globe. What we don't boast about is the smaller number of them who insist on evidential tongues. And of those that do insist on evidential tongues, we say little about the percentage who actually practice speaking in tongues.

There is a mushrooming growth of Christian people springing up who are "concerned primarily with the experience of the workings of the Holy Spirit and the practice of spiritual gifts." This spiritual hunger transcends denominational labels. In much of the world where the gospel is proclaimed, demonic activity is prevalent. More and more denominational missionaries are recognizing the necessity of having the Holy Spirit powerfully active in healings and exorcisms if they are to counter the influence of demonic powers. Here is a quote from the Lausanne Committee for World Evangelization: "A number of us, especially those from Asia, Africa and Latin America, have spoken both of the reality of evil powers and of the necessity to demonstrate the supremecy of Jesus over them. For conversion involves a power encounter. People give their allegiance to Christ when they see his power is superior to magic and voodoo, the curses and blessings of witch doctors, and the malevolence of evil spirits, and that his salvation is a real liberation from the power of evil and death." (From *Perspectives* on the world Christian movement, p. 518-519) More and more missionaries from various denominations ardently seek the Holy Spirit to empower them so they can be supernaturally equipped for power encounters with satanic forces. God is responding and vast numbers are being rescued from the dominion of darkness.

CHAPTER 10

ABUSE OF SPIRITUAL GIFTS

Since Scripture clearly does not support the teaching that evidential tongues must accompany every valid Spirit baptism, what is their purpose in this modern era?

In the past century there have been three major outpourings of the Holy Spirit in the United States. These outpourings occurred at Azusa Street in Los Angeles in 1906; in the Van Nuys Episcopal church with Dennis Bennett in 1960; among Roman Catholic students and professors at Duquesne University in 1967. Each was accompanied to some degree by speaking in tongues. The principle of Paul still holds true. Tongues were a progressive sign to unbelievers. And who were the unbelievers? In the United States, the cessationists in evangelical churches were the primary targets. And why weren't the cessationists convinced? Sadly, because of one erroneous doctrine which could not be supported by Scripture. And that doctrine is one that my denomination made its distinctive teaching: "Speaking in tongues is the initial physical evidence of the baptism in the Holy Spirit."

I have already demonstrated the inherent weakness of this doctrine and the fact that the purpose of tongues was totally misconstrued by Parham and then by others who followed his lead. The cessationists quickly pounced upon the weakness but they missed the real purpose of tongues:

(1) a sign that the supernatural work of the Holy Spirit was being revived within the church (Acts 2:17);

(2) a powerful symbol that no language group, nation or race was to be excluded from the fullness of the Spirit and salvation (Acts 2:21);

(3) a gift for communication with God, spirit to Spirit (I Cor. 14:2).

In order to combat what they correctly saw as error as far as tongues are concerned, they perpetrated an equally erroneous doctrine, namely, that the supernatural gifts of the Spirit were withdrawn from the church after the apostolic age. They tried to manufacture scriptural support for their tradition and twisted and contorted one or two texts beyond belief—although some will believe anything they think may lend support to a venerable tradition blessed by the elders. And that's where we are today, 2014. Until these issues are settled scripturally, the church in the United States will be unable to launch a counter-offensive against the spiritual forces that would destroy our witness to a society dangerously askew.

CESSATIONISTS POINT TO ABUSES IN PENTECOSTALISM

John MacArthur, Jr., in his book *Charismatic Chaos*, spotlights a number of abuses within the charismatic sphere. I know that much of what he writes has some validity somewhere within Charismatic and Pentecostal circles because I have seen it firsthand. MacArthur has done the church a service by pointing out serious flaws in various ministries under the umbrella of Pentecostalism. Ministries included in his critique of errors are personal prophecies, health and wealth proponents, and faith healers.

MacArthur's critique of faith healing reminded me of an event that occurred in Barstow, California. From 1970 until 1973, I was on the staff of the Commanding General of the Marine Corps Supply Depot in Barstow, California, serving as Depot Chaplain. This isolated desert community had an active ministerial association in which I participated, serving as president for a term. Through my association with the ministers, I became acquainted with a gifted young singer who was a member of a local Pentecostal church. I invited him to sing for the chapel congregation and our people loved his expression of gospel music.

In 1973 a healing evangelist came to town and this young man and his wife eagerly took their young son to the healing service to be prayed for. The youngster, perhaps eight years old, was afflicted with diabetes and was dependent on insulin shots. The evangelist prayed for the boy and declared that healing was assured to everyone who had faith to accept it. He then strongly admonished them to exercise faith for the healing of their boy.

The parents decided that as long as they were administering insulin to their child, they demonstrated a lack of faith.

Consequently, they quit giving him insulin and the child died. The parents were arrested and placed in the county jail in San Bernardino, facing manslaughter charges.

The young father later shared details of his tragic ordeal. His imprisonment was the least of his concerns. He was heartbroken over the loss of his son, and in utter despair he bared his soul to His Father. "Oh, God, I just wanted to demonstrate my faith in You and I thought You would be pleased. But instead, I brought reproach on Your name, my wife and I are disgraced, I am imprisoned—and my son is dead! Why? Why? Why?"

After he had poured out his heart, he became quiet in his spirit and God spoke to him. "My son, you were misled into believing that faith is preeminent. It is not. Love is the chief virtue and love always does what it can do for the beloved. Love demanded that you give your boy insulin and preserve his life. You withheld it and he died."

Elevating faith beyond its intent has been a trademark of many Pentecostal faith healers who capitalize on everyone's desire to be free from pain and sickness. Multitudes flock to healing crusades, believing the promise that they will receive healing if they will only believe. And on the flip side of that is the implication that if they are not healed, it is because they don't have enough faith. So the person that is not healed is not only left with his sickness, but also is burdened with guilt because of his lack of faith.

God does heal today, but not always. Paul left Trophimus sick at Miletus; Timothy was counseled to drink a little wine for his "oft infirmities", while Paul himself was made to endure his "thorn in the flesh." He endured it triumphantly after the Lord revealed its purpose. Paul also was instrumental in introducing vast numbers of people to spectacular healing miracles that captured their attention for the gospel. Jesus, the loving Healer, determines what is best for each in the light of eternity.

I am the oldest of eleven children, but three sisters and two brothers have preceded me in death. Earnest prayer was offered for the healing of each one. Three were taken from us while our mother was still alive and she stormed heaven on their behalf. There was no lack of faith before they died . . . or after . . . because our faith was in the Healer, not in the healing. They are with Him now, rejoicing together.

Just over four years ago, suffering from heart failure, I was on life support in the Intensive Care Unit of Madigan Army Medical Center in Fort Lewis, Washington. My attending physician, the head of the Department of Cardiology, told me later that he had doubts I would survive. A veritable hurricane of prayer was initiated on my behalf and those prayers, coupled with a skilled surgeon and a team of dedicated physicians and nurses, resulted in my healing. I am back again ministering in Ukraine, playing tennis and golf, preaching sermons, working in my office, gardening—everything I did before the crisis. Why was I healed and my much younger sisters and brothers were not healed? The Lord knows, and someday I will ask Him when "we talk it over in the by-and-by." In the meantime I continue life here, knowing the timing of my turn to join them is secure in the Lord's hands.

The sentence of physical death still hangs like the sword of Damocles over each head. "It is appointed to men once to die. . . ." The church's task is to anoint and pray and the Lord decides whom He will raise up. The Lord does heal, time and time again, but not always. I believe the local church should be the extension of Christ's healing hand to its community. We don't have to have the gift of healing to minister to the sick. Love always takes precedence over faith and we do what we can do. Jesus didn't say, "I was sick and you healed me." He said, "I was sick and you visited me." (Matthew 25:36) We dare not accentuate the spectacular at the expense of mundane acts of love unto "the least of these."

Godly Pentecostals deplore these abuses within their ranks. These are exceptions and not the rule. However, Pentecostals were "right on" with their emphasis on the experience of supernatural gifts of the Spirit signaling the imminent presence of God. In the face of ridicule and rejection they contended that God had not retracted the supernatural gifts from His Church. I believe the following four scenarios are examples of how spiritual gifts can be ministered effectively or, conversely, misused within the Church:

1) Spiritual gifts operated in love by Christians of unsullied character, who are filled with the Holy Spirit and display the graciousness of Christ as they minister, will powerfully advance the cause of our Lord and edify His church.

2) Gifts of the Spirit that may be genuine, but are wrought by Christians who are immature or unwise in the operation of spiritual gifts, may bring them into disrepute. This would include those described in 1 Corinthians 13 where gifts are manifested without love. Gifts of the Spirit apart from the fruit of the Spirit "profits nothing." The Spirit's gifts are truly gifts and, like all gifts, may be misused. Paul knows this and lays down guidelines for their use (1 Corinthians 14). The proper response is not to forbid the use of spiritual gifts but to teach the pertinent scriptural guidelines.

3) There are some Christians who, for whatever invalid motives, may actually try to effect sham spiritual manifestations. The apostles Peter, Paul and Jude speak of men who masquerade as believers but actually are deceivers. Paul calls them "savage wolves" who will come into the flock and wreak havoc These demonic manifestations infiltrate all churches, including Pentecostal groups (Acts 20:29-30).

I readily agree that all of these scenarios have been played out within the Pentecostal/Charismatic movement. But why dismiss the genuine because of isolated cases of the fraudulent? Is it a desperate effort to preserve a cessationist tradition at the expense of reality? This may be, but shouldn't be. In doing so, the cessationist created an atmosphere of needless antagonism.

The solid, mature, biblically literate representatives of the Pentecostal/Charismatic movement were not unaware of the danger of charlatans masquerading as agents of light. But it was difficult to defend against the broad-brush attack by fellow evangelicals and fight a rear guard action against false brethren at the same time. Defending the legitimate activity of the Holy Spirit was seen by opponents as attempts to give legitimacy to all that transpired under the umbrella of Pentecostal or Charismatic or Full Gospel. No one is more desirous of ridding their ranks of the spurious than the mature pastors and laymen who comprise the majority within the Assemblies of God.

After more than fifty years as an ordained minister within Pentecostal circles, I have seen the immature, the invalid, and the counterfeit displayed. On the other hand, no matter how genuinely endued with power or how gifted an individual might be, if he had not had an experience of being baptized in the Holy Spirit initially evidenced by speaking in tongues, we Pentecostals said he was not Spirit-filled and therefore not truly "spiritual." A spiritual caste system similar to that which apparently developed in Corinth developed in Pentecostal churches. I believe this itself is abuse of a spiritual gift. I have witnessed the pain it can inflict on those who earnestly seek to be filled with the Spirit but are not gifted to speak in tongues. This spiritual elitism is a dangerous blight upon the Pentecostal landscape.

COUNTERFEIT SPIRITUAL EMPHASIS

Sometimes this emphasis on speaking in tongues as the required initial evidence of baptism in the Holy Spirit led to unhealthy manipulation or even counterfeiting. Let me give an example which I personally experienced.

A well-known Assemblies of God evangelist was invited to speak at the church where I served as pastor in Northern California. I had not heard him preach but understood he had a gift for leading people into baptism in the Holy Spirit. Imagine my consternation and dismay when I discovered his methodology was to enjoin candidates to practice making nonsensical sounds with their tongue and lips as a prelude to being baptized in the Holy Spirit. To me, this teaching was blasphemous but apparently acceptable in some churches. I had to do "damage control" teaching and preaching to counter this ridiculous approach to a blessed and holy encounter with the Third Person of the Trinity.

I'm sure the Baptizer, the risen Christ, was grieved and dismayed more than I. But sincere, spiritually hungry seekers can rest confidently in these words of Jesus: *"Which of you fathers, if your son asks for a fish, will give him a snake instead? Or if he asks for an egg, will give him a scorpion? If you then, though you are evil, know how to give good gifts to your children, how much more will your Father in heaven give the Holy Spirit to those who ask Him!"* (Luke 11:11-13) The immature and misguided can be corrected with gentle, patient, biblical pastoral instruction. If one's heart is right, God will protect him from evil.

There is another unfortunate danger that lurks as a result of insisting that baptism in the Holy Spirit must always be initially evidenced by speaking in tongues. Sincere believers, if not provided mature, sound instruction, seek a baptismal sign rather than the Baptizer, a gift instead of the Giver. As a result, some considered they had spiritually arrived when they could testify to this experience and reveled in their new status. Fervor and enthusiasm are never legitimate substitutes for godly character and the gracious, palatable fruit of the Spirit.

I would be greatly misunderstood if it were concluded that I believe the abuses and excesses I have referred to characterize the Assemblies of God at their best. Not at all! I mention them because opponents who have seen these and other abuses refer to them as normative for Pentecostals. That is not true, particularly as the movement has matured. The vast majority of Pentecostal believers love the Lord, desire to live holy and productive lives in the power of the Holy Spirit, and to advance Christ's kingdom around the world. Nevertheless, there are substantive minorities that have built major belief systems out of isolated proof texts that remove them from the core teaching of biblical truth.

Following are three of the common misuses or abuses associated with speaking in tongues which I personally have found most onerous.

COACHING CANDIDATES FOR SPIRIT BAPTISM TO MUMBLE SYLLABLES IN PREPARATION TO RECEIVE THE SPIRIT

What a travesty! As if the Holy Spirit needed a coach to help Him do His work. Unfortunately, when tongues are made the required evidence of Spirit baptism, some eager proponents of evidential tongues concentrate on the "noise" rather than the "power." I was surprised to discover that this was a problem in the beginning of the modern Pentecostal era. Rev. E.N. Bell, first General Superintendent of the Assemblies of God, wrote an article in the denominational periodical decrying those who attempted to have people repeat certain phrases or words that would assist them to speak in tongues.

In all New Testament accounts of the outpouring of the Spirit, it is always a sovereign act of the Holy Spirit that usually occurs suddenly. Only once did candidates tarry and that was in obedience to Jesus' command to wait for the Spirit's arrival to coincide with the feast of Pentecost. Once it happened unexpectedly, to unlikely recipients, when soldiers of the Roman army garrison in Caesarea were baptized in the Spirit.

UNDISCIPLINED AND UNSCRIPTURAL USE OF TONGUES IN PUBLIC WORSHIP

I have seen biblical guidelines ignored because leaders thought they would be "quenching the Spirit" if they called misusers to task. Scripture plainly depicts how speaking in tongues is to be regulated in public worship. Those who speak in tongues can control where they speak and when. If they do not follow scriptural guidelines, leaders must enforce the apostolic instructions with tact, gently but firmly. If the correction is ignored, then the church must take more stringent action.

AN ATTITUDE OF SPIRITUAL SUPERIORITY DISPLAYED BY THOSE WHO HAVE SPOKEN IN TONGUES

The question in many churches became, "Have you received the Holy Spirit with the evidence of tongues?" rather than, "Have you received the Holy Spirit and experienced new power to express His gifts and fruit in your life?" Instead of a sign, tongues became the goal.

Although the Assemblies of God founders ignored scriptures that defined the purpose of tongues that accompanied Spirit baptism, they did understand that the supernatural gifts of the Spirit were being restored in a measure reminiscent of the book of Acts. This fact strikes at the heart of cessationism.

The gifts are in evidence in the Church today and there is overwhelming support in Scripture regarding their function. I have pointed out MacArthur's utterly weak attempt to enlist a scriptural text that supports his position. His attempt falls as flat as the Pentecostal's attempt to make tongues the undisputed initial evidence of Spirit baptism. Nor does MacArthur deal adequately with the historical fact that in every area of the earth and in every people group and church, the Holy Spirit gives supernatural demonstrations of the gifts of the Spirit to edify and build the

144

Church and glorify God.

DEMONIC ACTIVITY MASQUERADING AS TRUTH

I can recall only two instances in which I sensed demonic activity in the guise of a spiritual gift. Both had to do with the gift of prophetic utterance and both involved women claiming to have the gift of prophecy. They took place in the church where I served as pastor for nearly fourteen years. Let me share some of the history of what happened.

Upon retiring from the Navy chaplaincy, my wife Donna and I traveled for about a month, visiting family and friends and exploring new ministry opportunities. When we returned to California, I received an urgent call from the administrative office of the Northern California/Nevada District Council of the Assemblies of God. The Assistant District Superintendent wanted to see me as soon as possible. We met and he shared a sad story of a church that had potential but was about to die.

Several factors had brought about this near-death experience but, primarily, good pastoral leadership was lacking. In short, he persuaded me to consider becoming the fifth pastor in less than ten years to a small, struggling church in the East Bay area. Donna and I prayed about it, visited the community and the church site, and decided that the Lord was leading us to accept the challenge. On March 12, 1978, we conducted our first service. Despite a discouraged congregation, high indebtedness, and low financial resources, God began to revive spirits and build a church. Thanks to a handful of hardworking, visionary believers, we established a good name in the community and began to grow.

Growth brought some wonderful new converts into our fellowship. It also brought a few wandering stars from the charismatic orbit. One lady who showed up claimed to have the gift of prophecy. She would often take a prominent seat near the front, dressed all in white. One Sunday she stood dramatically and stated she had a prophecy for the church. I quickly sensed that she was not speaking under the inspiration of the Holy Spirit and asked her to be quiet. She flew into a rage, pronounced a curse upon me and the church, and exited the church, never to return. Such incidences are infrequent but when they happen, they provide the pastor an excellent opportunity to practice and teach biblical principles for Pentecostal worship. I was not sorry to see the lady in white depart; in fact, I felt greatly relieved to see her go.

The other instance of demonic influence was much more painful for me personally and for our congregation. As the church grew, we reaped a rich harvest of creative, intelligent members who were eager to get involved in advancing God's kingdom. A young couple joined us and quickly became involved. The wife had an executive position with an international corporation and was the family's major wage earner. They were childless but she had a gift for ministering to children. Our religious education director asked her to oversee our children's church ministry and it flourished under her leadership. She was popular and respected, and after being a part of the congregation for several years, she was elected a deaconess and served well. We had an active small group ministry in the church and this lady acted as a Home Group leader of about ten members who met weekly.

A few miles away in San Jose, a large charismatic church had developed a reputation for its promotion of the prophetic gift. Large numbers in the area were trooping in to hear and observe a prophet well known in some charismatic circles. Since I didn't move in those circles, I had scant knowledge of who was involved or what was happening. Our group leader apparently was intrigued by what she heard and decided to visit the church in San Jose, taking with her a few others who looked to her for leadership. They, too, seemed mesmerized by the "prophet," who specialized in personal prophecies directed toward individuals in the congregation.

Somehow, the group leader believed she was selected to exercise the gift of prophecy so as to predict events that would happen to individuals. She began to convey this to the Home Group, with mixed responses. The "select" ones who had accompanied her to San Jose were strong supporters, but others were definitely opposed and expressed their reservations. Mr and Mrs. Doe, probably in their mid-sixties, were particularly adamant in their opposition. Although they had not been church members long, they had sufficient maturity and knowledge of Scripture to recognize false teaching. The leader and her coterie were stymied by this opposition. (How could anyone be opposed to this manifestation of the Spirit?) This opposition soon came to a head in one of the home meetings. The "prophetess" announced that God had revealed to her that Mr. Doe was doomed to die in the near future.

At this point, Mr. and Mrs. Doe revealed to me what was happening in their Home Group and the role the leader played. Although they didn't believe the prediction was from God, they were shaken by it nonetheless. I was utterly dismayed by what had crept into our congregation. It was the heresy of Montanism revisited which I have addressed in an earlier chapter. As pastor I knew, of course, that those perpetrating this serious error must either repent or be removed—but first I had to allay the fears of these victims of a vicious demonic attack.

I led them to 1 Corinthians 14:3, the Scripture that provides guidance for judging prophecy. Here Paul gives three evidences of a true prophecy and we went over them together. First, true prophecy will edify, build up, or strengthen the hearer. Did the prophetic announcement do any of these? Obviously not. Second, true prophecy brings encouragement to the hearer. Were they encouraged by the prospect of dying soon? No, or we would not have been having that conversation. Third, true prophecy brings comfort. Were they comforted by the prediction of his imminent demise? No! This so-called "prophetic word" passed none of the scriptural tests for truth. It was not from God.

I encouraged this couple to relax and trust the Lord with their future. They should not, and need not, live in fear. This was the gist of my pastoral counseling and they latched on to it with confident faith. To my knowledge, Mr. Doe still lives over twenty years later.

My next task was a difficult but necessary one. I approached the leader with gentle firmness. She had been part of our church body and leadership team for several years and I respected her gifts and leadership qualities. I desperately desired her to acknowledge the error of her ways, repent, and be restored to fellowship. Instead, she displayed a haughty, superior attitude and repulsed my efforts. She also rejected the further efforts of the church leadership team to persuade her to submit to scriptural guidance. She insisted she had more authoritative guidance than the Bible, revealed to her personally by the Spirit. I knew it was a spirit but not the Holy Spirit that provided her guidance. Sadly, we had to remove her from the church.

Jesus said that one could tell the quality of a tree by its fruit. The fruit that followed this spiritual tragedy still grieves me whenever I think of it. The woman took a few people with her when she left the church and before long we heard reports that she was acting "weird." She wore eccentric clothing and let her hair grow long and hang down unattractively. Later, I heard she had shaved her head completely. Her husband divorced her and her "disciples" forsook her. I never had an opportunity to talk to her again and I have no idea of her current situation. I still pray for her when she comes to mind and I still grieve for her and for those she led astray.

I have related this incident because it shows what can happen when a Christian lets something other than Scripture become his "north star" for guidance. I am not a student of demonology or satanic activity but I firmly believe there are evil spiritual beings that are hell-bent on destroying people. Jesus combated them when He was here in the flesh. He even rebuked Peter for allowing himself to be deceived by Satan. That gospel episode in Matthew 16:21-23 is worth looking at in order to understand what took place with the woman described above.

Peter was essentially repeating one of the temptations Jesus endured in the desert after baptism. There He was offered kingship of the world if He would pay homage to Satan. What a deal. No suffering, no rejection, no cross. In return He would be handed the world on a silver platter. He could use His power to force His subjects to serve Him, but Jesus rejected it out of hand because He was playing for much higher stakes. His kingdom was not of this world nor was it tainted with this world's value system. Peter didn't yet understand this and he became Satan's mouthpiece. He wanted the plaudits of men, a position of power, an absence of suffering . . . and he wanted Jesus to supernaturally provide it right now.

The woman in our church was satanically deluded by the glitz surrounding what purported to be a prophetic gift. The prophet was honored as if he were a spiritual superman. I think she wanted what Peter desired and for the same reasons. Once she let her own desires supersede scriptural guidelines, she was in need of rebuke.

And when she rejected a scriptural rebuke from the body of Christ, she left herself open to destructive demonic activity.

Paul understood the reality of evil spiritual forces. He wrote to the Ephesian church: *"For our struggle is not against flesh and blood . . . but against the powers of this dark world and against the spiritual forces of evil in the heavenly realms."* (Ephesians 6:12)

Likewise, he warns Timothy: "The Spirit clearly says that in later times some will abandon the faith and follow deceiving spirits and things taught by demons. Such teachings come through hypocritical liars, whose consciences have been seared as with a hot iron." (1 Timothy 4:1-2) Obviously, these "hypocritical liars" are in the church system or those with faith would not be threatened. No religious system or denomination is exempt from this threat.

I am completely confident that God has restored the gifts of the Spirit to his church. Nevertheless, I am very much aware that counterfeit and demonic deceptions are also possible. The Scriptures above clearly indicate the apostolic church faced these, as well. But the apostles didn't discard the gifts of the Spirit because they were sometimes counterfeited, and neither should we. Instead, the apostles gave us scriptural guidelines for ministering the gifts and preventing their abuse. The fact that I had not been able to prevent a valued member of my congregation from being deceived and then leading others into deception played heavily upon my mind and heart.

On the last Sunday of November, 1991, I preached my final pastoral sermon and helped the church install the new pastor. In a few weeks I would celebrate my sixty-fourth birthday. Donna and I were in good health and both convinced that God had something further for us to do. Little did we know that the Holy Spirit would lead us into an exciting and completely unforeseen ministry . . . on the other side of the world.

CHAPTER 11

RACISM WITHIN
THE PENTECOSTAL MOVEMENT

I said earlier that one purpose of tongues at Azusa street was to be a sign to cessationsists that the supernatural gifts of the Spirit were being restored to the church. The cessationists missed the sign, partly because the Pentecostals assigned an erroneous significance to tongues that was not clearly supported by Scripture. As a result, the cessationists not only rejected the sign but also the reality of the spiritual gifts to which the sign pointed.

The outpouring of the Spirit accompanied by tongues conveyed a sign to unbelievers. Who were these unbelievers and what didn't they believe? None other than white Christians who didn't believe blacks should be welcomed as equals into the Christian community. This sort of racial bias was true in the first century and the twentieth. The early church, comprised of Jewish believers, was convinced that all Gentiles must convert to Judaism before they could join their fellowship. It wasn't until Peter heard Gentile soldiers speak in tongues at Caesarea that he understood the significance of what happened at Pentecost. Tongues were God's sign that He would not tolerate racism in His family.

It was no accident that God chose a half-blind, African-American pastor to lead the revival on Azusa Street. Racism was still rampant in America less than fifty years after the Civil War. People of color, particularly blacks, were still treated as second-class citizens by white Americans. When the revival at Azusa Street was launched, powerful demonstrations of God's power drew people from all races and walks of life. They worshipped together; they cried together; they laughed together; they were one in the Spirit together. For a short time there was genuine evidence of the equality of people groups within a Christian community.

The worldly culture, immersed in prejudice and racial bias, was quick to condemn the interracial demonstrations of Christian unity. One Los Angeles newspaper spoke of the "disgraceful intermingling of the races" and described Pastor Seymour disparagingly as a "one-eyed, illiterate Negro." The beautiful spirit of unity and harmony at Azusa Street began to crumble under the onslaught of racism. But it wasn't external racism that produced the collapse of mutual love and respect. Prejudice imbedded in the church brought about the ignominious failure of this attempt by the Holy Spirit to create interracial harmony. The church had missed the sign.

One of the great "what-ifs" of the last century is: What if the church had not missed the sign of racial unity and equality tongues was meant to convey? Fifty years of humiliating abuse and injustice to our black brothers could have been averted. Race riots of the fifties and sixties could have been prevented as black and white Christians reached out together to transform our racist culture. We missed the sign and instead interpreted tongues as physical evidence that individuals had been filled with the Holy Spirit. They had been filled with the Holy Spirit, but the purpose of the Spirit was to empower them to help bring about racial equality just as the Spirit did in the first century.

Sadly, the chief perpetrator of racial bias came from within Pentecostal leadership ranks. It was Charles Parham who mentored William Seymour, son of a former slave, and taught him that tongues were the initial physical evidence of being filled with the Holy Spirit. When Parham heard of the great revival taking place in Los Angeles under the leadership of his former pupil, he went to investigate.

Parham was repulsed by the intermingling of the races. Also, he apparently was jealous of Seymour's place of leadership and tried to assert his authority over that of the black pastor. Fortunately, this was resisted not only by Seymour but by the congregation. Parham left and later wrote scathing attacks against the intermingling of the races such as he had witnessed in the Azusa Street revival. He described it as a "horrible, awful shame." The negative criticism by Parham birthed further criticism by whites, and the grand potential of Christian racial unity came to nothing.

Parham is falsely depicted by some as the father of the Pentecostal movement. I believe he is the father of the erroneous teaching that the baptism in the Holy Spirit must be initially evidenced by speaking in tongues. This "evidence" or "sign" was not for the believers who had been baptized in the Spirit. As Paul stated, it was a sign for unbelievers. A sign of what? Most of those baptized in the Spirit at Azusa Street were African-Americans. Some, like Pastor Seymour, were children of slaves. When the Spirit filled them and they spoke in tongues, God was giving evidence that this people group were first-class children in His family and must be treated with respect. And who were the "unbelievers"? Why, of course, prejudiced white Christians who had adopted the culture of the world.

In 1948 the Assemblies of God was involved in the formation of the all-white Pentecostal Fellowship of North America. There were no black Pentecostal churches invited to participate. I was a twenty-year-old airman stationed at Hickam Field, Hawaii, at the time. That year President Harry Truman signed the executive order that integrated the armed forces of the United States. I remember well when the transition was made and my barracks welcomed black men for the first time. It had been legal to die together, now it was legal to live together. If the church ignored the Spirit's mandate to break down racial barriers, then the Spirit would employ government force.

A friend of mine, Dr. Ron McConnell, a charismatic Episcopalian minister, related the following incident to me. At the time of the incident, he was a young Air Force chaplain ordained by the Assemblies of God. He attended the 1957 Assemblies of God General Council in Cleveland, Ohio, and was present when a delegation from the Church of God in Christ presented a proposal to the Council that the Assemblies of God and the Church of God in Christ unite their denominations. The leaders of the Assemblies of God quickly spoke against this proposal and it died. Today in the United States the Assemblies of God is struggling to maintain the status quo and the Church of God in Christ continues to grow toward six million members. How sad that we once again ignored this opportunity and pulled about us our robes of spiritual and racial superiority.

I became very painfully aware of the curse of racial prejudice within the church when I was senior chaplain at a Marine Corps Air Station in South Carolina during the mid-sixties. We had a thriving congregation of Marines and I loved ministering to them. An outstanding black officer and his family had joined our chapel congregation soon after being transferred from Hawaii. After attending the chapel for several months, the young officer and his wife came by to see me.

"Chaplain," they said, "we love the chapel services but we live off the base in town. We would like to get involved with a local church in the civilian community. In Hawaii we attended a Pentecostal church and enjoyed worshipping there. Can you recommend a Pentecostal church for us to attend?"

Without really thinking I immediately recommended the local Assemblies of God church. Sometime later I was mortified to discover that the church which I had recommended had treated this family deplorably. They shunned them and let them know that they were not welcome. I was angry and terribly disappointed. Our General Superintendent visited me shortly thereafter and I told him what had happened. He soothingly counseled me, "Now, Chaplain, these church people are fine folks. You have to understand their culture and accept them as they are. If I were to reproach them for their actions, we would likely lose a church." I was wounded by his words and lost some respect for our national leadership. Most of all, I ached for that black family . . . still do.

The Assemblies of God has made giant strides since the incident described above. In 1994 in Memphis a historic gathering now called the "Memphis Miracle" occurred. Here at last black and white, Pentecostal and charismatic, heard what the Spirit was trying to convey to the church at Azusa. Black Pentecostal and charismatic leaders joined with white Pentecostals and charismatics in an effort to bridge decades of racial separation.

The Roman Catholic participation in charismatic renewal had spurred some interracial interaction as far back as the 1970's and 1980's. But Memphis was different. Careful planning, much prayer, and shared responsibility preceded this momentous event. A white Assemblies of God pastor and a black Church of God in Christ pastor co-chaired the planning committee that did the hard work before the event began. Both had been pastors in Memphis for twenty-nine years, yet they had never met one another before their work on the planning committee brought them together.

From the moment the participants gathered, there was an air of expectation. The speakers bared their hearts, not glossing over hurts given and received, acknowledging injustices and sinful behavior. They wept together, they asked forgiveness of each other, they laughed and rejoiced together. God did a significant work of inner healing. Before the "Memphis Miracle" concluded, a new organization had been formed called Pentecostal and Charismatic Churches of North America. It comprised a cross section of Pentecostal and Charismatic believers across the continent, regardless of race. There was a long way to go but, under the direction of the Holy Spirit, the racial barriers were coming down. This is part of what the sign of tongues is all about.

I rejoice that the Northern California/Nevada District, to which I have belonged for nearly forty years, has made significant strides forward in race relations. Samuel Huddleston is a dynamic black preacher who serves as the Assistant District Superintendent. The School of Urban Missions in Oakland is a cooperative effort between the Church of God in Christ and the Assemblies of God. Together they provide an outstanding training program for developing ministers to serve the inner cities.

Although the Assemblies of God initially missed the significance of tongues relating to race relations, they were more alert regarding the sign pointing to restoration of the gifts of the Spirit. One thing the Church can thank the Pentecostal movement for is that they demonstrated that the gifts of the Spirit, with supernatural manifestations, were operative in the church again.

This question comes to mind: If the Assemblies of God erred so badly in interpreting the significance of tongues, why has God blessed them as He has? First, growth is not necessarily a proof of divine approval or blessing. If it were, I could name some cults that are marvelously blessed. Most of our growth has been overseas where we have fostered unity among different people groups, which has produced extensive growth. Perhaps the primary reason God has blessed us despite doctrinal error is because we have exalted and preached Christ as Lord, Savior, Baptizer and coming King.

God will bless whoever exalts His Son, regardless of imperfection in the witness. The apostle Paul recognized this as he pointed out the imperfection of some witnesses who opposed his ministry because they were jealous. Isn't Paul's gracious spirit amazing in the following passage?

"It is true that some preach Christ out of envy and rivalry, but others out of good will. The latter do so in love, knowing that I am

put here for the defense of the gospel. The former preach Christ out of selfish ambition, not sincerely, supposing they can stir up trouble for me while I am in chains. But what does it matter? The important thing is that in every way, whether from false motives or true, Christ is preached. And because of this I rejoice." (Philippians 1:15-18)

He rejoices because the gospel is proclaimed and God will bless the proclamation even though the proclaimer exhibits error. God blesses the Assemblies of God despite error just as He blesses many other denominations who proclaim Christ but have some error in their traditional belief system. The Apostle Peter is a dramatic example of a Pentecostal preacher who won thousands to Christ before he ever understood the meaning of tongues at Pentecost. It took years before the significance of Joel's prophecy penetrated the barrier of his biased religious tradition.

Our country faces tremendous destructive pressures, both internally and externally. International terrorism has made the United States its number-one target. Internally, we have an education system being highjacked by materialistic humanism; rampant hedonism manifesting itself in drug addiction, illicit sex, gluttony and pornography; an economy ravished by greed and mismanagement by big business and big government; and the entertainment world and mass media with all its sordidness and twisted values. Our national culture is honey-combed with sordid morals and sabotaged by a philosophy of godless materialism.

Paul declares in 2 Timothy 3:1 that in the last days *"perilous times will come."* But they will also be days of great opportunity for the gospel. The gifts of the Spirit operating in all the church can provide the spiritual, emotional and intellectual stimulus that will produce positive Christian options. Sanctified and energized imaginations with persistent hard work, employing all the spiritual resources God has provided through the gifts as well as the fruit of the Spirit, can accomplish results that are otherwise impossible.

The big question is, can we Christians meet the challenges the world hurls at us? We can do so only if we remember the purpose of the Spirit's presence among us. In Luke 4:18-19 Jesus pinpointed this in His first sermon after returning in the power of the Spirit following His temptation. His text was from Isaiah 61:1-2: *"The Spirit of the Lord is on me, because he has anointed me to*

155

preach good news to the poor. He has sent me to proclaim freedom for the prisoners and recovery of sight for the blind, to release the oppressed, to proclaim the year of the Lord's favor."

Jesus' fellow townsmen were favorably impressed with the first part of His sermon. However, when He pointed out that God had chosen foreigners to be the recipients of special favor, they became murderously belligerent and drove Him out of town. God's love and compassion for the starving widow of Zarephath and the diseased Syrian general could not change the mind-set of a people committed to their tradition of racial superiority. They angrily rejected this part of Jesus' sermon and drove Him from their midst. The good citizens of Nazareth missed the opportunity of a lifetime—to their eternal shame.

The Spirit's visitation at Azusa Street resulted in a similar rejection of Jesus' message and for the identical reason. What the Spirit through Jesus could not do at Nazareth He also could not accomplish in Los Angeles, namely, destroy the corrosive attitude of white superiority ingrained by long tradition into the white culture. Our white Pentecostal forebears also missed an opportunity of a lifetime—to their lasting shame. Harvey Cox described it this way, *"Finding that some people could speak in tongues and continue to abhor their black fellow Christians convinced him (Pastor Seymour) that it was not tongue speaking but the dissolution of racial barriers that was the surest sign of the approaching New Jerusalem. The early white Pentecostals disagreed. Uncomfortable under black leadership and embarrassed by the opprobrium heaped on them for 'worshipping with niggers,' they finally opted to reject interracial fellowship and keep the tongues."* Harvey Cox, *Fire From Heaven, p.63.*)

I cannot cast stones. I may even have joined them had I been there at that time. Sometimes the Spirit frees us instantly from the enslaving attitudes imposed by tradition, as with Saul of Tarsus. Sometimes we struggle and tenaciously resist for a lifetime. But the Spirit does not give up on us. He is the Spirit of new beginnings.

The Holy Spirit had to thrust us out to Africa, Asia and South America to discover the truth we had rejected at home. Most of the growth in all these areas is the result of dedicated native citizens taking spiritual leadership and reaching out to their own people.

Wherever the growth was greatest and most enduring was where the white missionary assumed the role of servant and helper.

Harvey Cox, the aforementioned insightful Harvard theologian who investigated us Pentecostals, had some words of warning and words of encouragement. First, his words of warning:

"I was disillusioned to find that some believers in the movement that had been born in a stable were now being seduced by preachers who told them that God wanted them to have dominion over everything. I was infuriated by preachers who were telling trusting and vulnerable listeners that if they were poor or not in perfect health it was their own fault for not having enough faith. I was exasperated at the way sleazy values of the rich and famous had seeped into Pentecostal worship. . . . Most of the Pentecostals I knew personally were as outraged by all this as I was. But I was not at all sure that even the most courageous of them could put up the kind of battle that seemed to be needed in their churches.

"I began to harbor the sad suspicion that the Pentecostal movement that I had come to admire in my reading of its history and in my visits to other continents might be destined for an endless splintering into mean-spirited factions headed by power-obsessed egoists in the country of its birth. I feared that it might lose touch completely with its humble origins and become the righteous spiritual ideology of an affluent middle class. But then it occurred to me that almost all the unsettling experiences I had had in the Pentecostal world had been in largely white settings.... It began to appear more and more certain to me that American Pentecostalism has paid a very high price for its racial divisions. In 1907 William J. Seymour, the moving spirit of the Azusa Street revival, wrote in the mission's newspaper The Apostolic Faith:

"'Tongues are one of the signs that go with every baptized person, but it is not the real evidence of baptism in everyday life. . . . The secret is: one accord, one place, one heart, one prayer, one soul, believing in this great power. Pentecost . . . brings us all into one common family.

"'But this ideal faded quickly. The revival that one visitor said was a demonstration of the power of the Spirit to "wash away the color line with the blood of the cross," and to purge the church of the sin of the racism, had resegregated itself very quickly. Today

Pentecostalism stands in grave danger of losing the invaluable message it could bring to the other churches and to the rest of the world. What had happened to the spirit of Azusa Street?'" (Ibid. p. 296-7)

What happened is this: God intended tongues to signify that all the language groups of the world were eligible to be filled with His Spirit and receive salvation, as the prophet Joel declared (Acts 2:17-21). This sign was necessary to break Judaism's control on the gate leading to salvation. Instead of proclaiming this unifying purpose, Pentecostal leaders made tongues the necessary evidence of valid Spirit baptism. This created a spiritual caste system that undermined the Divine intention of tongues. As a result disunity prevailed.

Cox goes on to say: *"Answers to the questions about what experience is and what the Spirit is doing in the world will not appear first in journals but in the ways these little outposts of the kingdom live in a world that is both hostile and hungry. The reason I am hopeful that Pentecostalism will emerge from the current fray on the side of the angels comes not principally from what I have read, but from what some of these outposts, especially a very small but very symbolic one, are actually doing."* (Ibid. p. 319-20)

Cox then goes on to describe a small congregation in Dorchester, a section of Boston overridden with crime and degradation. The group owns no building but rents a hall in which to meet. The members are young black Pentecostals, many of them graduates of elite colleges in the Boston area. They have determined to invade "the gates of hell" in the power of the Spirit and plant an outpost for God's kingdom.

He depicts the service he visited this way: *"They know about early Pentecostalism and with a finely honed sense of history they call themselves the 'Azusa Christian Community.' The day I visited the regular Sunday worship . . . the members sang with gusto, shook tambourines, and worshipped with infectious jubilation. But what impressed me most was the intensity of their prayers. . . . They prayed that God would touch the hearts of the drug dealers who pandered their wares openly just down the street so they would see the error of their ways. They prayed for the sick, including, when I requested it, my sister-in-law who was suffering from leukemia. But they also prayed for lab projects, and finding a job.*

"Here were people who had chosen to be actual witnesses to the kind of community their Pentecostal ancestors foresaw. But they know they cannot do it without each other's support or without prayer. The Reverend Eugene Rivers, who leads the congregation, makes the rounds of the Massachusetts Institute of Technology, Harvard, and Boston University, challenging young graduates to forego moving to the suburbs and to join the Azusa Community on the urban frontier. 'But if you don't pray,' he warns them, 'don't come.'" (Ibid. p. 320-21)

THE INTERRACIAL MINISTRY OF FAITH BROWN

I could have shared with Professor Cox an even more dramatic story of Spirit-filled young people in action. My sister, Faith Brown, was a young school teacher in Springfield, Missouri, in 1968. The Holy Spirit directed her to go to New York City and assist in fulfilling David Wilkerson's dream of establishing a Spirit-directed ministry to "one of the most drug-infested, poverty-stricken ghettos of New York City—Fox Street in the heart of the South Bronx."

Continuing from the foreword by David Wilkerson in the book *An Uncommon Faith* by Carol Brown Patterson: *"I sought to staff this ministry by appealing to some of the brightest and most idealistic young people in the nation, young people hungry for a challenge to flesh out a practical, life-changing Christianity. The conditions of employment in this ministry, CURE Corps (Collegiate Urban Renewal Effort), would scare away all but the most dedicated and stable young Christians. But it appealed to a revolutionary, sold-out young maverick for Christ—Faith Brown."*

Faith soon became a leader within CURE Corps, advancing to become its Director. She loved the people of Fox Street with a supernatural love, although at first they didn't trust her. Her blue eyes and blond hair advertised she was a hated "whitey." Some vilified her, some threatened physical harm, and many just tried to ignore her. But Faith refused to be ignored. Together, she and her black, brown and white colleagues kept knocking on doors, inviting parents to bring their children to the free, private school that CURE Corps had established. Through their ministry of love to the children, they eventually won the respect and trust of the community.

Faith immersed herself in the culture of the downtrodden in New York City. She joined Bethel Gospel Assembly, a black church in Harlem, whose pastor, Bishop Ezra Williams, was a remarkably astute and open-hearted leader. He soon discovered that my sister's love for his people was genuine. Pastor Williams' warm acceptance of Faith led the people to trust her so much that she was democratically elected as Youth Leader of the church. Incidentally, Pastor Williams' son was the other nominee. She also was chosen to serve as an Elder and helped form policy for the church.

Faith's lasting monument to her interracial ministry is Urban Youth Alliance International. This ministry started as the result of a young Pentecostal Puerto Rican named Ben Alicea who formed Seekers Christian Fellowships on the campuses of New York University and Bronx Community College. Soon Christians on other campuses began inquiring how they might establish chapters. Eventually Seekers chapters were established on numerous high school and college campuses.

In 1978, Urban Youth Alliance International was incorporated as a 501(c)(3) nonprofit to provide support and leadership for Seekers and other developing ministries. Faith Brown served as the first Executive Director, Ben Alicea as Chairman of the Board and Pastor Williams as Vice-President. The ministry flourished under Faith's leadership until her tragic death in 1988. Dr. Austin Akalonu became "interim" Director and served until 1994, when the Reverend Wendy Calderón Payne, a Colombian-American, resumed the leadership as Executive Director. Seekers Clubs are now found on approximately twenty-five NYC high school and college campuses. UYAI has numerous other pro grams under indigenous leadership that are making a difference in New York City. These are led by Spirit-filled believers dedicated to the task of making Christ's love tangible and personal as they minister "to the least of these, my brothers."

Faith has always been an inspiration to me. Her ministry was far more difficult than mine, and more significant. She was sixteen years younger than I and I adored her when she was a little tyke, so shy and loving. But I wanted to get to know her better as an adult and an opportunity presented itself in 1988. Donna and I were hosting another tour to the Holy Land and Faith agreed to accompany us. I procured her ticket and eagerly looked forward to our time together, but it wasn't to be. Five years after deadly breast cancer had been arrested, it metastasized and she became too ill to make the trip. Not many weeks after our return from Israel, our family gathered in New York City to attend her funeral service. As we gathered together in Harlem inside the sanctuary of Bethel Gospel Assembly, we listened reverently as this great black church extolled the character and ministry of their beloved "Sister Faith." It was a beautiful homegoing celebration, full of tears . . . and laughter and music.

A statement by Faith testifies to her theology and life: *"Involvement with Christ demands an involvement with human need. You will find yourself the possessor of the power that equips you to meet human need. You can and do get involved—not just because it is the humanitarian thing to do, but because you have an answer. The power of the Holy Spirit can direct you daily to human need and, through sharing this power, the needs are met. Drug addicts are cured, confused persons do find direction and beauty in life, love for everyone is possible."*

My sister Faith saw clearly many years ago what I have just begun to see in the process of writing this book. The Holy Spirit outpoured at Azusa Street was directing us to human need embodied in other people groups, especially blacks and Latinos. We rejected the real message and substituted another that continues to bring hurtful division within the body of Christ.

Can God work in this for good? I believe He can, but on His terms, not ours. There must be confession, repentance, reconciliation and acceptance. Pentecostals, of whom I am one, should initiate this process. If we dare to do so I believe the genuine supernatural fire of Pentecost will be rekindled. It will burn up the divisive, the trite, the false and counterfeit, the abuses and misuses. Its flames will burnish the glow of holy love and integrity of character. Jesus' prayer that His followers may *"be brought to complete unity..." (John 17:23)* will be one glorious step closer to fulfillment.

CHAPTER 12

WHERE DO WE GO FROM HERE?

Do we really believe that God answers prayers that are prayed in accordance with God's will? Do we acknowledge that Jesus' prayer in John 17 is in accordance with God's will? If so then we must surely believe that someday the church will experience unity such as has not been known since the first century.

What has prevented that from happening? I am convinced it is because the church has refused to hear or heed the message the Holy Spirit is conveying when tongues are outpoured. The cessationist fundamentalists declare that the Holy Spirit has ceased communicating as He formerly did. The Pentecostals misinterpret the sign and make it the evidence of Spirit baptism rather than the symbol of the universality of the gospel for all language groups around the world.

REVIEW AND APPLY SCRIPTURAL PRECEDENTS

We have examined the historical record of the outpouring of the Holy Spirit in the early church and these truths are clearly depicted:

• There was no set pattern that dictated where, when or how the Spirit was outpoured or upon whom.

The Holy Spirit demonstrated His sovereignty by taking action as He deemed appropriate. He alone can read the hearts of people and He determined true candidates to be endued with power from on high. I conclude we should continue to submit to the Spirit's sovereignty.

• Sometimes Spirit baptism occurred before water baptism, sometimes after. Sometimes there was laying on of hands, sometimes not. Sometimes it was preceded by a sermon, sometimes not.

Clearly the Spirit wanted to establish precedents that showed this was a sovereign work of God and not something dictated by religious ritual or tradition.

- Except for the one hundred twenty obeying Christ's command to wait in Jerusalem, there is never any hint that people tarried or sought the baptism in the Holy Spirit.

There was a time lapse between water baptism and Spirit baptism for the Samaritans but there is nothing to indicate they were seeking the baptism in the Spirit. I have offered a reasonable explanation for the delay. The Spirit always chose the time, the place and the recipients.

- In some instances languages unknown to the speakers accompany the outpouring of the Spirit.

In keeping with the prayer and intent of Jesus, this is a sign to promote unity in the body of Christ among divergent people groups. As demonstrated in the early church, this divinely ordained sign, which pointed back to Pentecost, promoted unity and demolished racial bias among diverse people groups.

- The Spirit's sign can be ignored or misinterpreted.

We see this happening at Pentecost as well as at Azusa Street. The Jewish disciples at Pentecost, and all were Jews, ignored the sign of tongues that pointed to the universality of the gospel across all cultures and language groups as Joel stated. They were not ready to deal with their biased religious tradition.

The founding Pentecostals after Azusa Street were entranced and beguiled by spectacular experience which became the foundation for their theology. They misinterpreted the purpose of the sign of tongues and brought schism into the body of Christ.

- Whether or not one speaks in tongues when Jesus outpours the Spirit will be determined by the Spirit Himself. Many times when racial prejudice and tribal animosities are barriers to unity (such as in Africa), this sign can convince the recalcitrant that his "enemy" is really his "brother." When the Spirit is sovereignly acting, there will be no doubt that the power of God is being displayed.

- We must genuinely trust the Holy Spirit to provide the utterance when He desires tongues to be manifested.

He needs no one to coach, entreat, or coax someone as a prelude to speaking in tongues. When the Holy Spirit is the initiator, He will choose the right persons, the right time, the right setting and the "unbelievers" who need convincing. God always knows what He is doing.

WHAT CONCLUSIONS SHOULD WE DRAW FROM THESE PRECEDENTS?

• We should restore the gift of speaking in tongues following Spirit baptism to the Spirit's sovereignty.

He alone knows the thoughts and intents of the heart and when this sign is necessary to promote unity in the body of Christ among different people groups. When the Holy Spirit does this as a sovereign act, there will be no doubt of God's presence and power.

• To continue to ignore or misinterpret the sign of speaking in tongues will continue to promote disunity and delay the answer to Jesus' prayer.

Chapters 14-17 of John's gospel comprise the "last will and testament" of Jesus. The ministry of the Holy Spirit is directly tied to the fulfillment of His prayer. Just as the Holy Spirit had united Jesus to His disciples and to the Father, so the Spirit is promised to unite all who will believe in Jesus "through their message." Would the Spirit choose to manifest Himself in a way that the assumed purpose of the manifestation would result in disunity and fragmentation of Christ's body? I do not, I cannot, believe this to be true.

USING TONGUES FOR PERSONAL EDIFICATION

If you greatly value the gift of speaking in tongues during your prayer times, as I do, you may think that the manifestation of this gift will drastically decrease if we acknowledge that it is not the initial physical evidence of Spirit baptism. Not so. I believe speaking in tongues in one's devotional life will significantly increase. I believe many of those who formerly rejected speaking in tongues, because they saw the unscriptural application to Spirit baptism, will be hungry for any help the Holy Spirit can give them to enhance their relationship with God and build them up spiritually. Paul says two things that are apropos here.

"For anyone who speaks in a tongue does not speak to men but to God. Indeed, no one understands him; he utters mysteries with his spirit." (1 Corinthians 14:2)

Sometimes when I go to prayer I am overwhelmed with the complexity of situations and simply do not know how to pray. I can pray in the Spirit, sing in the Spirit, and refresh and build up my spirit. My confidence in God is renewed as I focus on Him and I am reassured that no situation is too complex for Him.

"He who speaks in a tongue edifies himself." (1 Corinthians 14:4)

To edify means to build up. It connotes growth and development leading to a fuller expression of the character of Jesus Christ. I need all the help I can get in being built up and growing and reflecting more of the image of Christ.

As Christians see how this gift enhances spiritual growth, there will be a new openness, even hunger, for this manifestation of the Spirit. Of course, we are built up in order to make us more effective in manifesting other gifts which are designed to edify the whole body of Christ.

I am encouraged by the fact that many, if not most, in the Pentecostal/Charismatic orbit today do not demand evidential tongues as proof of Spirit baptism. After I resigned from the Assemblies of God in 2010, I affiliated with a charismatic chaplains' organization that proclaims and practices the spiritual gifts bestowed by the Holy Spirit but does not teach or demand evidential tongues. Spirit-filled chaplains associated with Chaplaincy of Full Gospel Churches are ministering in the power of the Holy Spirit in the U.S. military, in prisons, in hospitals, in retirement communities, in police and fire departments and wherever God opens a door of service.

I am not suggesting a change just because we are out of step with global Pentecostalism. I am urging we change our position because we are out of step with Scripture. We must change because we are contributing to disunity within the body of Christ. Dare we do it? Or will we stumble along, crippled by increasing schism and alienation?

"My prayer is not for them alone. I pray also for those who will believe in Me through their message, that all of them may be one, Father, just as You are in Me and I am in You. May they also be in Us so that the world may believe that You have sent Me. I have given them the glory that You gave Me, that they may be one as We are one: I in them and You in Me. May they be brought to complete unity to let the world know that You sent Me and have loved them even as You have loved M.e" (John 17:20-23)

Jesus' prayer recorded in John 17 still awaits its fulfillment. These words reflect our Lord's deepest desire. They should fill our hearts with sorrow because we have failed so dismally. They should fill us with hope because there is still opportunity to bring them to fruition. May His Spirit open our eyes to the path that leads to unity within the Body of Christ.

I know my sojourn on planet Earth is almost completed—more than fourscore years are behind me. I realize that I could be face to face with my Lord at any time. I yearn to see the whole body of Christ come together so that the world knows that Jesus truly is from God. I believe Pentecostals can and should take the lead in bringing about reconciliation. We should confess that we have been divisive, however inadvertently that may be for many. Our doctrine has been based on a tradition that grew out of a mislabeled experience and has become encased in a burgeoning bureaucracy, and only the Holy Spirit's power can free us so that we can advance rather than hinder the answer to Christ's entreaty.

The Assemblies of God, peopled by those I love and respect, cannot undo the response of the early leadership following Azusa Street, but we can redo it. How so? We can acknowledge and repent of our failure to heed the Spirit's voice. The Holy Spirit called us to reject our inherited racial tradition and accept and affirm our black, yellow, and brown brothers. We clung tenaciously to our old tradition and rejected our brothers and sisters, and then we constructed a new tradition that became our "distinctive." The very sign of speaking in tongues that was to herald the good news that another people group was to be welcomed into the church, "with all the rights and privileges thereto," became a divisive distinctive instead. Our racial bias has changed dramatically for the better in many areas but we need to change the doctrine that originally contributed to it.

Some will object, "If we acknowledge that we missed the Spirit's intent for tongues, it will be the death of the Assemblies of God." No, never! It will not be the death—it will lead to a glorious resurrection. Of course, there can be no resurrection without a prior death. If we do not face this issue head-on and take Spirit-led corrective action, I believe our church will continue in the doldrums. But, if we confess we got off track, it will make headline news across Christendom; TV talking heads will begin discussing the new emphasis that promotes unity within the body of Christ. People will flock into our churches, eager to associate with a church body that demonstrates a spirit of humility and seeks forgiveness for past error. The Holy Spirit will be accorded His sovereignty, and a huge breach within the church will be healed. We Pentecostals/Charismatics have been accused of elevating personal experience above divine revelation as final authority. This action should put that charge to rest.

Peter responded to the question concerning the meaning of tongues at Pentecost by quoting the prophet Joel, a portion of which is: *"Your young men will see visions, and your old men will dream dreams."* (Joel 2:28)

At 86 years of age, I qualify as an old man. Allow me to share my dream with you. I have a dream for the Assemblies of God, the church with which I was associated for over fifty years. A dream that her young men and women will catch a vision of what might be if their church were not bound by the tentacles of a "distinctive" based on assumptions and tradition rather than the clear teaching of Scripture.

I have a dream of another reformation in which devout Pentecostal and Charismatic believers, laymen and Bible scholars, follow the example of the Bereans who *"received the message with great eagerness and examined the Scriptures every day to see if what Paul said was true."* (Acts 17:11) I have a dream that multitudes will see that being part of the answer to Christ's prayer is far more important than adhering to a questionable denominational dogma.

I have a dream that bureaucratic inertia and pride will not prevent corrective action being taken regarding our position on speaking in tongues. I have a dream about the tremendous blessing of God that will follow if we humbly acknowledge our mistaken dogma. I have a dream of multitudes flocking into a church that is honest and capable of confessing past mistakes.

I have a dream that unparalleled manifestations of the gifts of the Spirit will be displayed in materialistic America as they are in China, Korea, South America, Indonesia and throughout Africa. The genuine miraculous demonstration of God's power will counter humanistic claims that supernatural events are impossible. I have a dream that when tongues are no longer a sign of spiritual eminence the temptation to counterfeit or feign evidential tongues will be removed and a hunger for the genuine will emerge.

I have a dream for my cessationist brethren, a dream that when your Pentecostal brothers confess that their tradition about the purpose of tongues is mistaken, it will free you to confess that your tradition about the gifts of the Spirit is also mistaken. I have a dream that your confession will free the Holy Spirit to manifest His gifts more freely among you, bringing great blessing to all God's people.

I have a dream that the supernatural manifestations of the Holy Spirit will be numerous and authentic so as to undermine the power of secularists. I have a dream about cessationist scholars and Pentecostal scholars, Protestant charismatics and Catholic charismatics, white and black and brown, being able to sit down and talk regarding the Holy Spirit's supernatural activity in the church today. I have a dream that the world will be impacted by this sign of unity within the church, that our Lord will be exalted and the church will multiply. I have a dream that the sovereign activity displayed by the Baptizer at Caesarea will be rekindled again and again around the world.

I may not live to see any of my dreams realized, but I believe it will happen. Something such **as** I have dreamed must come to pass. How else can a fractured church regain its integrity? How else can the supernatural activity of the Holy Spirit be released in all its power? How else can we begin to actuate Christ's prayer for unity?

I believe even now that the Spirit is stirring hearts and minds to bring together the body of Christ. Somewhere there are young men and women who will see a vision of what I dream about.

Someone has to take the leadership.

Who will it be?

POSTSCRIPT:
THE SAGA OF FRED BOSWORTH

Fred Bosworth was an early Pentecostal leader who was tremendously respected for his integrity and ministry gifts. He was a gifted musician, church planter and hugely successful evangelist. Thousands testified that they were healed as a result of God's answer to his prayers. Until I began research for this book, he was a complete stranger to me. Now, I must confess, he is one of my heroes. Because of his importance as a founding father of the General Council of the Assemblies of God, a brief biographical sketch is appropriate.

Bosworth was born on a Nebraska farm near Utica on January 17, 1877. His father was a Union Civil War veteran. As a youngster he attended a veterans' reunion with his father where a cornet was played. He fell in love with the instrument, which led to a lifetime devotion to music, both instrumental and vocal. He excelled as a band musician while in public school, advancing to a leading role in the Nebraska state band.

His future as a musician was seriously threatened when he developed lung problems when he was about eleven years old. It persisted for eight more years and his health deteriorated. Doctors diagnosed tuberculosis and predicted he would die soon. Fred had committed his life to Christ at age sixteen so he was spiritually prepared to die. However, he wanted to visit his parents before death claimed him. His parents had moved from Nebraska to Fitzgerald, Georgia, where a subsidized Union veterans' community had been established.

Bosworth was near death when he arrived but his mother nursed him to health to the degree that he was no longer housebound. He attended a church where divine healing was preached. He was prayed for and God healed him. With his health restored, he decided to settle in Fitzgerald. He successfully engaged in business and won the respect of the community. He ran for the office of city clerk and served a two-year term. While serving as city clerk he was married, in 1900, at the age of twenty-three. He retained his enthusiasm for music and formed and played in a band until his religious convictions about some situations led him to resign.

About 1901 the Bosworths saw copies of a newsletter distributed by John Alexander Dowie, the leader of a religious community that had founded the town of Zion, Illinois. Dowie was a complex and talented religious leader and an important figure in the early history of modern Pentecostalism. Dowie promoted the gift of healing and thousands claimed they had been healed under his ministry. In 1899 he purchased sixty-five hundred acres of rural land along Lake Michigan north of Chicago. At the turn of the century he made public his plans for building Zion City. A year and a half later the city was prepared to receive six thousand new settlers. At this time the Bosworths made their move to Zion City. His musical ability was quickly recognized and he was soon installed as band leader of the city.

Dowie was an eloquent and persuasive speaker and people came in droves to hear him. However, he rapidly lost his popularity when he began to display bizarre and erratic behavior. In June, 1902, he declared himself Elijah and assumed the brilliant and costly dress of Israel's ancient high priests. His popularity continued to drop when he spent vast sums on a worldwide evangelistic tour, even though he was facing bankruptcy in Zion City. In 1905 he suffered a stroke while in Mexico. While he was gone, Zion City voted him out of office and Wilbur Voliva was chosen to replace him. A year later another massive stroke took his life.

In 1906, while Zion was going through its leadership crisis, Charles Parham visited Zion and presented his view of speaking in tongues as the required evidence of Spirit baptism. The Pentecostal teaching by Parham thrived in the fertile soil at Zion. Supernatural gifts of the Spirit, particularly healing, paved the way for the expectation of other spiritual gifts, particularly of languages spoken under the inspiration of the Spirit (tongues). Fred Bosworth, the popular and talented band leader of Zion City, was very interested in the message proclaimed by Parham. He hungered for an empowering experience from God. He was baptized in the Holy Spirit accompanied by speaking in tongues during Parham's 1906 visit to Zion City.

There is no indication that Bosworth had a preaching ministry while in Zion. However, he used his popular role as a band leader as a platform for personal witnessing. This no doubt helped him develop his successful preaching ministry. In 1907 Bosworth began conducting evangelistic services. He grew rapidly in spiritual stature as God blessed his ministry with many converts. In 1910 he started a thriving Pentecostal church in Dallas, Texas, which he later transferred into the Assemblies of God.

In 1914 Bosworth attended the first General Council at Hot Springs, Arkansas, which gave birth to the Assemblies of God. He had been appointed to serve one year as an Executive Presbyter. He was thoroughly Pentecostal, convinced that God was restoring the supernatural gifts of the Holy Spirit to prepare His people for Christ's return. However, as he traveled extensively, preaching at numerous Pentecostal gatherings, including revivals, conferences and camp meetings, he became troubled about the doctrine that insisted that every valid Spirit baptism must be verified by speaking in tongues. His search of Scripture led him to conclude there was no biblical basis for this teaching. Furthermore, his observations convinced him that it promoted a "gift" instead of the "Giver," that it tended to result in "shallow" baptisms, and that it was the source of confusion. Bosworth further rejected the distinction Pentecostals tried to make between "evidential tongues and the gift of tongues: He wrote a persuasive tract and began to circulate his views" (*The Assemblies of God*, Blumhofer, p. 240)

The editor of the official periodical for the new denomination, *The Christian Evangel* (later, *The Pentecostal Evangel*), filled its pages with articles written by prominent Pentecostals who favored the "tongues as evidence" position. Bosworth's writings were excluded since the editor opposed his position. The power of the negative press made it impossible for Bosworth to get a wide or fair hearing. Bosworth saw that Parham's theory of the purpose of tongues had been adopted by the leadership of his church. Rather than continue to fight against a position he saw as deeply flawed, with no foundation in Scripture and the source of needless division within the body of Christ, he submitted a letter of resignation. He expressed regret for having to leave the fellowship he helped establish but he would not, could not, compromise his convictions. He wrote a letter July 24, 1918, to J.W. Welch, an Assemblies of God leader: *"If I had a thousand souls, I would not be afraid to risk them all on the truth of my position that some may receive the fullest baptism in the Spirit without receiving the gift of tongues."*

(A/G archives, Ibid. p. 241)

Although Bosworth resigned from the Assemblies of God, he remained firmly committed to the empowering experience of Baptism in the Holy Spirit. But he saw clearly the error in and danger of making tongues a required validation of Spirit baptism. He warned: *"Error in teaching is another cause of trouble and is mainly responsible for so much of the superficial work and consequent irregularities which Satan has used to turn aside thousands of hungry souls. The purpose of this letter is to point out what I consider a serious doctrinal error, the elimination of which will solve many of our difficulties, besides opening the way for more of the manifestations of the Spirit and a much deeper work of God. The error to which I refer is the doctrine held by many, that the baptism in the Spirit is in every instance evidenced by the physical sign of speaking in other tongues as the Spirit gives utterance, Acts 2:4, and that this is not the gift of tongues referred to in Paul's writings to the Corinthians (1 Cor. 12). After eleven years in the work on Pentecostal lines (during which time it has been my privilege to see thousands receive the precious baptism in the Holy Spirit) I am certain that many who receive the most powerful baptisms for service do not receive the manifestation of speaking in tongues. And I am just as certain many who seemingly speak in tongues, are not nor ever have been baptized in the Spirit."*

Through all the controversy he remained intensely loyal to the reality of Spirit baptism and the endowment of supernatural gifts. He knew these were abundantly supported by Scripture and he had seen them in his own ministry. He was passionate about adhering to the truth of Scripture and equally passionate about rejecting the unbiblical. Before I discovered Bosworth's article "Do All Speak With Tongues?", I was sure there must be a divine purpose for tongues that accompanied Spirit baptism at Pentecost and subsequently. I was frustrated in not being able to discover a biblical reason for the gift of tongues. After prayer and continued searching, God began to remove the scales from my eyes. I came to see that my question must have been the same question the apostles wrestled with. Where would they have looked for answers? In Scripture, of course. The only Scripture available to them was the Old Testament.

What Old Testament Scriptures deal with the meaning or purpose of tongues? I could find only two, but they were definitive. One was from the prophet Isaiah, loosely quoted by Paul in the context of First Corinthians 14:20-22. The other is from Joel, quoted by Peter at Pentecost. A careful exegesis of these passages convinced me that tongues accompanying Spirit baptism have two purposes. First, Paul extracted from the Isaiah passage this principle: *"Tongues are a sign, not to believers, but to unbelievers."* (1 Corinthians 14:22)

The Joel passage quoted by Peter reveals that the gift of tongues was a symbol of all the languages of the world which the gospel must penetrate in the power of the Holy Spirit. Sadly, Parham and his followers chose a theory based on personal experience rather than divine revelation as their basis for doctrinal truth. Personal experience must be solidly based in Scripture before serving as a basis for inerrant truth. If not, the inevitable result is disunity and abuse of the experience.

Bosworth clearly saw the danger of the Parham position. Following is Bosworth's cogent application of Scripture to the issue of tongues. (I wish I had discovered this before my first edition of *Pentecost Revisited.*) He writes: *"The doctrine that all are to speak in tongues when baptized in the Spirit is based entirely upon supposition without a solitary 'Thus saith the Lord.' It is nowhere taught in the three instances recorded in the Acts they spoke in tongues as a result of the baptism. While this notable fact should serve as an eye-opener to those who contend against any speaking in tongues, it is by no means conclusive proof that God gave the same gift to all the multiplied thousands added to the church during this most marvelous period of church history extending over more than a quarter of a century.*

"God always has a definite purpose and an infinitely wise reason for everything he does. The day of Pentecost witnessed the grandest and most effective display of the gift of tongues the world has ever seen. And God's purpose was that it should be a 'sign,' not to believers, but to the unbelieving Jews dwelling in Jerusalem 'out of every nation under heaven.' God's purpose was most wonderfully realized. Three thousand unbelieving Jews were, by the fact that these Galileans spoke in their own languages, forced to believe that Jesus was actually the Messiah. Perhaps there was

173

no other sign that God could have manifested so effectively under these circumstances as speaking in tongues. Eight years later Peter and the six Jewish brethren who accompanied him to the household of Cornelius, with all other Jews, unbelievers all to the Gentiles being included to the privileges of the gospel. So God made His gift of tongues a sign to these unbelieving Jewish Christians, thus convincing them, to their astonishment, that 'God also to the Gentiles hath granted repentance unto life.' When Peter returned to Jerusalem, the apostles and brethren contended with him, saying, 'Thou wentest in to men uncircumcised, and didst eat with them.' So Peter rehearsed the matter from the beginning and closed his argument by saying, 'As I began to speak, the Holy Ghost fell on them, as on us at the beginning.' If the thousands who were saved during the wonderful revival period of eight years between the second and tenth chapters of Acts, spoke in tongues when baptized in the Spirit, why should he point back only to the time when they spoke in tongues on the day of Pentecost? Again, eight years later, when Paul met the brethren at Ephesus who had never heard there was any Holy Ghost, God gave them both tongues and prophecy when they received the Spirit. And if Luke was so careful to record it when these few spoke in tongues, why did he not record it when all the many thousands since Pentecost spoke in tongues, if they all did?"

No wonder the "tongues as evidence" proponents who founded the Assemblies of God wanted to silence the voice of this Spirit-filled man who insisted that Scripture and reason not be usurped by experiences and assumptions. As I read Bosworth's defense of his position, I came across nuggets of truth that I had not considered. Here is one example. "The word 'evidence' in the Scriptures is never used in connection with a spiritual gift, or manifestation, making faith to depend upon any sign or physical manifestation, but the Apostle distinctly states that 'faith is the evidence.' Anything that is to be received in answer to prayer is to be received by faith, even the great miracle of the new birth, and Paul expressly states that we are to 'receive the promise of the Spirit through faith.' Galatians 3:14. Nothing short of faith can satisfy the heart and give us power. Paul said, *'Let everything be done with a view of building up faith.'* But this teaching reverses this, not only destroying faith, but making it impossible until the*

174

gift of tongues is received."

This great Pentecostal minister of a century ago concluded his fifteen-page open letter with this paragraph: "*I find that by standing right with the Scriptures, with regard to all these manifestations of the Spirit, our revivals are deeper and quicker, and we will be free from many of the irregularities and much of the fanaticism that has torn up our work and hurt the cause of God in so many localities. I have been waiting for some of the other Pentecostal brethren to come out with literature on this line, but I guess they have been a little timid, like myself, so I have felt it my plain duty to my brethren to write this for their perusal. I know I will lose the friendship of some who may not be able to see the truth herein contained, but if I can be of help to others, opening the way for their greater usefulness, I will feel well repaid. I am sure if our movement could be free from this one error in teaching, and would preach the greater things about the baptism, our opportunities for usefulness would be increased manifold. The way would be opened for more manifestations or gifts of the Spirit, and consequently the revivals would be greater and deeper.*"

My heart resonates with this brother from a past generation. I understand his disappointment that no influential Pentecostals had come to the fore in behalf of presenting a purpose for tongues that is solidly based in Scripture. I understand his disappointment when Pentecostals adopted a theory about the purpose for tongues that has produced division within the body of Christ. I am grateful that Fred Bosworth insisted on making Scripture, not experience, the ultimate test of doctrinal truth. Scripture affirms the gift of tongues but never affirms tongues as evidence of Spirit baptism.

Thank you, Fred Bosworth, for affirming that truth a century ago. I wish I had seen it sooner.

More

from

this

Author

If you want more insights into Pentecostalism, read the prequel to this book, Pentecost Revisited... And be sure to read R. Glenn Brown's next book, Ukraine Adventure, where the author shares his years of ministry in this critically important nation.

Do you have a ... story to tell?

Port Hole Publications
is seeking entertaining, educational,
wholesome material to publish.
let us know if you have the next
great novel languishing in a drawer,
a personal memoir or researched
topic to print.

Contact us through our website:
PortHolePublications.com

We bring over 40 years of
experience to our projects.

CPSIA information can be obtained
at www.ICGtesting.com
Printed in the USA
FFOW05n1454250414